Footprints on the Sands of Time

by

Don H. Loftin

To Geof Schwer my friend & fellow co-worker who assisted in transformation of James Connally Air Base into the James Connally Technical Institute. Now TSTI

DHL 8/30/18

Footprints on the Sands of Time

Copyright 2006 by Donald Howard Loftin

All rights reserved. No part of this book may be used or reproduced in any manner whatsoever without written permission of the author except in the case of brief quotations embodied in critical articles or reviews.

Published in the United States of America

DEDICATED TO

Don, Tim, and Shane for helping make the journey through life of your mother and me a joyful and exciting experience. May this history and genealogy serve as a bridge to your Loftin ancestors in America.

ACKNOWLEGEMENTS

I was fortunate to establish lines of communication with several genealogists during my search for Loftin ancestors none more helpful than Arnold Loftin, Rosepine, Louisiana and Ashley Loftin of Albuquerque, New Mexico. We soon discovered a common ancestor, Benoni Loftin 1705-1755 North Carolina, grandson of Leonard Laughton (Loftin) founding father of the Loftin name in America. Benoni served as the focal point in retracing our lineage to Leonard Laughton (Loftin) who settled in Henrico Province of Virginia in 1636. Martha Johnson of Palacios, Texas connected me with Arnold Loftin who had copies of family records of Asa Loftin our great great grandfather. Additional info came from State Archives in Jackson, Mississippi and Raleigh, North Carolina. A wealth of information on the Loftin family in America is on file and available from those depositories. Too numerous to list were numerous state and county records which provided essential data toward completion of the history of my Loftin family in America entitled Footprints on Sands of Time.

Special thanks to my wife, Sissie, for listening to endless hours spent correcting and revising passages as new information became available. Also my deepest appreciation my daughter-in-law, Diana Michelle Loftin, for endless hours spent editing and shaping Footprints into presentable form.

Don Loftin
Spring Lake
2008

INTRODUCTION

Seems hard to believe over a quarter of a century has passed since the publication of The Loftin Chronicles June 1982 the result of years searching for my Loftin ancestors. My goal in the beginning was finding the birthplace of my grandparents, Leonard Lee Loftin and Frances Collins. My father and other siblings were told they came from somewhere around Jackson, Mississippi. Apparently none of the twelve siblings attempted to retrace their parents' trail, especially Jane and Amanda the two oldest born in Mississippi. If they had knowledge of this nature it went to the grave with them. Dad said they were too busy. He had a good point! Their days were devoted to making a living.

My search for family roots, from 1979 through 1982, led through eight generations of my Loftin family in America. This was the data that went into the first edition of The Loftin Chronicles in June 1982.

Copies of the Chronicles were printed and made available to those attending the annual Loftin reunion July 10-11 1982 at Honey Island, Texas. Descendants of Leonard and Frances Loftin came together most from southeast Texas however other states were represented including Louisiana, Mississippi and Ohio. At the time, my interest was in making this information available to family and close kinsmen so no copyright had been obtained consequently copies were reproduced and found their way into hands of genealogists throughout Texas and much of the south who have contacted me for information regarding their family lineage. Some I could and did provide data which proved helpful. Ironically with the advent of the personal computer and the Internet thousands suddenly began searching for their ancestral roots. The Chronicles became quite popular as a source of Loftin genealogy not only in America but on the continent as well.

The 1982 reunion near Honey Island was held in an area of Hardin County where Leonard and Frances Loftin along with Elizabeth Dyess Loftin his widowed mother and other kinsmen put down roots after arriving from Mississippi. My great grandmother Elizabeth and four of her sons settled within a twenty mile radius of Honey Island in communities of Thicket, Saratoga, and Votaw. Elizabeth in her late sixties at the time lived out her life around Honey Island and was buried nearby. Her grave disappeared through years of neglect. Several of her children, grandchildren and great grandchildren are buried in Felps Cemetery in the Thicket community ten miles northwest of Honey Island.

Copies of an old portrait of my Loftin grandparents were available to those attending. They were an impressive couple. Except for a few older most had never seen a picture of those early pioneers who came on oxen drawn wagons to this area in 1873 from Mississippi. This was truly a historic occasion for their descendants. It is good to know the reunion continues today thirty years later in various locations about the state. Not many Loftins left of those attending the reunion at Honey Island in 1982.

I was personally pleased to share my findings with so many kinsmen especially my sister, Doris Loftin Parker, brothers, Leonard Harmon Loftin and George Calvin Loftin and their families. Our brother James Lee

Loftin had passed away three years before in June 1979 however his widow, Irene Swain Loftin, and their two children, James Lee Loftin, Jr. and Lissa Ann Loftin were present.

The search, which ultimately led me through eight generations of my paternal ancestors, began as a search for the birthplace of my grandfather Leonard Lee Loftin. In August 1979 my family was living on the Texas State Technical College campus near Waco, Texas where I was a member of the administration. A neighbor, an avid genealogist, suggested I send a letter of request to the Supervisor of Archives in Jackson, Mississippi regarding possible info on file regarding my grandfather.

I sent this request and a week later received the following information: a copy of the 1850 Federal census of Jasper County, Mississippi showing Ezekiel A. Loftin(46) head of household, Sarah (wife) sons, Andrew, Ezekiel, John, Giles, Thomas and Leonard (my grandfather) one year.

I now knew the county where my grandparents came from along and also names of my great grandparents Ezekiel (1804) and Sarah Loftin. Included was a copy of a marriage license issued to Leonard Lee Loftin and Frances Abigail Collins in 1868 in Jasper County, Mississippi along with a copy of a genealogy written in 1936 entitled Loftins and Allied Families of North Carolina by Mr. and Mrs. M.E Creasey of North Carolina. Each of these items proved helpful and motivated me to search for the next link of my ancestral chain my great great grandfather Loftin.

I continued searching for additional ancestors in America and Europe with little success however managed through a stroke of good fortunate to establish lines of communication with Dr. J A. Lofting Norwich, England who had done extensive research of his name in England. His search revealed the following derivatives of the name: Lofting, Loftings, Loftingh, Laughton and Loftin. This name change was of considered help inasmuch as Leonard Laughton is considered the founding father of the name in America.

How Dr. Lofting and I managed to enter into correspondence is another story. Simply as a result of a neighbor a Mrs. Monica Taylor who was a native Englander. She gathered names of Loftins from kinsmen in England each of whom I wrote to describe my genealogy quest for

Loftins. One of those whom I wrote forwarded the name and address of Dr. Lofting who had recently phoned him for such information. The connection was made. The letters between us over the next two years proved important in the finalizing of the history of my Loftin family in America later on. He and I shared a common belief a member of the family fled England during a religious persecution and settled in Holland. A member of this family married into Dutch blood and in time a descendant of this family returned to England.

So the search which began for the birthplaces of my Loftin grandparents ultimately led me through eight generations of my family in America. Along the way I compiled a file of credible data which encouraged me to write a history spanning eleven generations of the family from the founding father to my grandchildren. It is given the title Footprints on Sands of Time.

It seems as though in every tribe, family and or generation one is called to find ancestors, to put flesh on their bones and make them live again. To tell the family history and story and in so doing somehow know they know and approve. We are the story tellers of the tribe called as it were by our genes. Those who have gone before cry to us: tell our story. So we do!

Don H. Loftin
Spring Lake
12/28/ 2000

Eleven Generations of
My Loftin Family in America

(1) Leonard Loftin (Laughton)*
Born: England 1616(circa)

(2) Leonard Loftin*
Born: Pennsylvania 1654

(3) Benoni Loftin*
Born: North Carolina 1705

(4) Ezekiel Loftin*
Born: North Carolina 1750

(5) Asa Loftin*
Born: North Carolina 1784

(6) Ezekiel A. Loftin*
Born: Georgia 1804

(7) Leonard Lee Loftin*
Born: Mississippi 1848

(8) Leonard Harrison Loftin*
Born: Texas (Thicket) 1887

(9) Don Howard Loftin
Born: Batson, Texas 1925

(10) Don H. Loftin
Born: Lafayette, La. 1947

(10) Timothy Howard Loftin
Born: Beaumont, Tx.1956

(11) Timothy Cole Loftin
Born: Fort Worth, TX. 1989

(10) Shane Stephen Loftin
Born: Corpus Christi, Tx.1961

(11) Lance Tyler Loftin
Born: Waco, Tx.1986

FORWARD

For reasons known only to a good and merciful Lord I have been on my journey through time ninety years and counting. As far back as I can remember there was this hunger to know who my ancestors were both paternal and maternal.

My Zorn grandparents lived long lives well into the 1960's consequently I was able to enjoy learning something of their family history. This was not so with my paternal lineage as my Grandparent Leonard Lee Loftin died in 1923 two years prior to my birth. My grandmother, Frances Collins Loftin, died in 1935 when I was circa eight years old. My time with her was limited however very few eight year olds are concerned with genealogy at that age. Too many other things have more priority. Unfortunately I was never to learn family history at the knees of these grandparents.

They had twelve children two in Mississippi ten in Hardin Co Texas. The eighth being my father Leonard Harrison Loftin. My Loftin grandfather died of a stroke at his home in Cleveland in 1923. Three items owned by my grandfather ended up in my father's possession: two smoking pipes (one tobacco sack) also a large picture of my grandparents in a silver frame. There was also a hand written record by Leonard Lee Loftin of his family names and dates of birth. In time these all came into my possession except the pipes. The written record proved important later on.

My Loftin grandparents raised twelve children in the Thicket settlement in Hardin Co Texas three of which died quite early: Ezekiel only seven and sisters, Lydia and Matilda both relatively young women. So that left nine who grew up in the thicket. One James Millard at age of nineteen rode up to Trinity County near Pennington and worked for a man named Sheffield. The man wanted to sell so Millard apparently convinced his parents to buy the Sheffield place. In 1904, Leonard and Frances sold out in Thicket and moved to Trinity County with four of their younger children: Leonard Harrison, George Willis, Sabre Palley and Benjamin Hector. Remaining in the Thicket were Stacey Artist married to Alice Marcontell, Willard Wiley, Paula Jane, and Frances Amanda married to Swearingen brothers.

Leonard Lee and France's Loftin with all of their children except Millard now rest in Felps Cemetery. Several of the children lived long lives so it seemed logical to assume some must have left some record of where Leonard and Frances lived prior to moving to Texas. If such information existed, I never found it. Of course my father was the main source I went to for family history but his response was my parents with my two older sisters came from Mississippi probably around Jackson. That was all I had to go on until I was married with three sons when something happened in June 1979 which led me to seriously search for my Loftin ancestors. Actually I only wanted to find the birthplace of my grandparents which shouldn't have posed a problem. After examination of the birth records of the children I was certain the move took place between 1871 and 1874 probably in 1872.

The determination to begin the search for my Loftin roots came during the gathering of our Loftin families for the final services of my brother James Lee Loftin at his home in Sour Lake Texas June 22, 1979.

Relatives from Hardin Co and surrounding counties came some not seen for decades. My brother was well known having served Hardin County as commissioner after returning from captivity as a prisoner of war in Germany during WWII .Pilot of a B17 shot down over Denmark on his 13th mission. Married with two children active in community, church and politics. So the turnout for his final services was quite clear large. We laid him to rest in Forrest Lawn in Beaumont then returned to his home to spend time with his widow, Irene and children Jim and Lissa Ann.

During this time several of the younger members began asking the same question I posed to my dad as a boy "Where did our Loftin ancestors come from?" We older ones could only say somewhere around Jackson we were told. This wasn't satisfactory to the youngest who begin offering their opinion as to the origin of their ancestors. Their opinions focused not on Mississippi or any of the states but England, Wales, Norway, Holland and Switzerland. Most based on their reading of history

Such confusion convinced me it was time to get answers to this question. Prior to departing my brother's home several of our group agreed to drive to Jackson Mississippi later that summer to search the records hopefully for information about our grandparents. Fortunately, this trip proved unnecessary.

A day or so after returning from my brother's services while engaged in talk with a neighbor I mentioned the proposed trip to Mississippi in search of information re my grandparents. He smiled then asked "Why don't you forward a letter of inquiry to the Supervisor of Records or Archives in Jackson, Mississippi? Enclose a self-addressed stamped envelope." I did.

Within a week I received back from Jackson a large envelope containing the following data: 1850 federal census of Jasper, Co Mississippi showing the household of Ezekiel A Loftin, Elizabeth (wife) and sons, Andrew, Ezekiel, John Thomas, Giles, and Leonard (my grandfather), as well as a copy of a marriage certificate for Leonard Lee Loftin and. Frances Abarilla Collins dated June 16, 1868. Wow. This information was easily obtainable for anyone making the effort. With minimum effort on my part, I found the county my grandparents came from along with their dates of marriage and the names of my Great Grandparent Loftins. I informed my brothers and sister, who were in disbelief until they saw the data.

These findings provided the motivation to continue the search for more Loftin ancestors. In the following months I was fortunate to discover several genealogists searching for their Loftin lineage among them Arnold Loftin of Rosepine, Louisiana, Ashley Loftin of Albuquerque, New Mexico and Mrs. Charles Johnson of Palacios, Texas. It was this lady who referred me to Arnold who then introduced me to Ashley Loftin who had amassed a great amount of genealogical material on the Loftins in America. Arnold and Ashley and soon discovered we had a common ancestor in Benoni Loftin of North Carolina.

I sent letters to State Archives in Raleigh, N C for information on file regarding Benoni Loftin and received several items of interest: the will of Leonard Loftin (1654) resident of Albemarle, NC describing possessions he wanted to leave to his children. Also a copy of a genealogy entitled Loftin and Allied Families of North Carolina by the Creaseys of N.C. These items along with the wealth of data contributed by Arnold and Ashley encouraged me to write the genealogy of my family entitled The Loftin Chronicles.

I presented a rough outline of the work to members of our Loftin families attending the Loftin Reunion at Monsanto Park, Alvin, Texas in July 1981. The decision was made then to have the next reunion at Honey Island for descendants of Leonard Lee and Frances Collins Loftin who settled near this site after arriving from Mississippi. We were reaching out to their descendants, many still living in and or near this part of the state. In some, first cousins were living within ten miles of the site for the reunion. This reunion was scheduled for July 11-12 on grounds of the Honey Island swimming pool.

During this time I was employed by the technical college near Waco, Texas supporting a wife and three sons so completing the Chronicles and getting it into printable format before reunion meant extra work on the weekends. Fortunately the Chairman of our college print shop saved the day by not only putting the work into printable format then running off one hundred copies. To top it off he added an interesting cover with a picture of a black panther to each copy.

While this was going on a local artist friend of mine refurbished an old portrait of my Loftin grandparents really in terrible condition. He did a tremendous job. Not only redid the portrait as to same size but added smaller prints eight by eleven. So by reunion time I was ready armed with the copies of The Loftin Chronicles and small portraits of Leonard Lee and Frances Loftin.

Regarding the large redone portrait I had received approval from the director of the Big Thicket Museum in Saratoga, Texas to accept the portrait of my grandparents for hanging in a prominent place in the museum. We were ready for the reunion, expectations high, prominent guests invited. I was to serve as moderator and introduce guests then present the history of the family to those assembled.

On the Saturday prior to the Sunday reunion several members of our immediate family met at the Big Thicket Museum in Saratoga where I in behalf of our parents Leonard Harrison and Jimmie Lois Loftin and deceased brother, James Lee Loftin, presented the picture of our Loftin grandparents to the curator who promised a prominent place on the wall of the museum. We were glad to do this, but within five years, the museum closed due to lack of funding support. All possessions had to be reclaimed so Sissie and I, during a visit to see my brother Leonard Harmon in a nursing home in Kountze, TX, went by and got the picture. It's now in our home here on Spring Lake.

The reunion went well the following day with well over a hundred and seventy five some from out of state showing up. Copies of the Loftin Chronicles were distributed along with small pics of the Loftin grandparents. I wasn't aware those Chronicles were soon reprinted and passed into the hands of family members who did not attend the reunion. I wasn't aware this had happened until I began receiving calls from people requesting assistance whose kinsmen had married into the Loftin lineage.

The gates had been opened for the distribution of The Loftin Chronicles over a great part of the nation.

The chronicles began appearing in several states. I then realized an author only has control of his work through copyright, which never entered my mind. I was eager to get the work to family and kinsmen. So if my research with considerable help from others helped someone discover their family lineage it was worth doing.

In the years following the 1982.Reunion I continued the search for ancestors in England using Leonard Laughton (Loftin) as the focal point. I was able to contact Dr. John Loftingh who was researching the family history in England to determine if certain illnesses he had treated were hereditary. His research covered several centuries if English history revealed his Loftingh name underwent numerous changes over time among these: Loftinghs, Lofting, Loughton, and Laughton and Lofton.

We shared a common belief that during an early period of religious persecution a family named Lofting fled from England to Holland where a family member married into Dutch blood. A member later returned to England where, in time, other derivatives appeared, among which were the Laughton or Loftin name. This was branch which produced the Leonard Laughton (Loftin) who came to Virginia in 1636. This is the first Loftin name appearing on records in America. The name Robert Laughton appeared on a ships log a year or so later thought to be a brother.

As my research continued through the 1980s and '90s so did the accumulation of information regarding the particular period of time in which each ancestor lived. A review of the data convinced me a comprehensive history of my Loftin family was possible forming a bridge between my grandchildren and the founding father of the Loftin name in America. The first draft of my work entitled Footprints on Sands of Time was completed circa 2006, however, revisions continued with revelation of information regarding my Collins ancestors of Jones County, Mississippi the birthplace of my grandmother France's Collins Loftin.

Don H Loftin

Chapter One
The Founding Father
Leonard Laughton* (England)
1616-1675 circa

"During the early years of the seventeenth century hundreds of Englishmen came to the Virginia Colony in America and they came for various reasons. Regardless of status -all English born-English bred -resolved to be Englishmen forever, but once they set foot on the shores of this land they knew it not but they'd not be Englishmen again!"

~Anonymous Source

During the month of July 1636, an English ship entered the southern reaches of Chesapeake Bay from the Atlantic continued across this expanse of water and entered the mouth of the James River. The ship three months out of Southampton was loaded with material and supplies for large plantations along the upper reaches of the James engaged in the production of tobacco for the humidors of London. The ship after unloading cargo at Jamestown continued upriver dropping off cargo at West and Shirley One Hundred, Diggs One Hundred and Upper One Hundred farm settlements along the river. Eighty miles or so above

Jamestown in the Henrico Province the ship docked to unload material and equipment for Elisabeth Parker owner of five hundred acres of farmland on both sides of the James along with eleven men, nine white, two black, under contract to work for Mrs. Parker. The record of this is found in the records of James City Virginia and the Virginia Magazine of History and Biography, Volume 5, Page 343. The records read: "Elizabeth Parker, widow, five hundred acres in the county of Henrico, between Cules and Varinas, bounded on the south by this main river, and on the east by Four Mile Creek, due in right of her late husband, Sergeant Sharpe, who, as appears by certificate of Henrico Court Dated 25 April 1636 transported nine workers and two Negroes, 12 July 1636 by West." I assumed West was the ship bringing the workers to the colony however later found out West was the governor of the Henrico Province responsible for approving all cargo and personnel arriving in his province.

The names of those on the roster who came to work for Mrs. Parker were: Richard Vase, John Thomas, Lewis Jones, William Cooke, Peter Whidbey, Edward Jones, Jon Ward, William Cooley and Leonard Laughton. (The name underwent several name changes through the centuries we discovered later through correspondence with a Doctor J. Lofting in Nor fort England including the name Loftin.) Since this is the earliest Loftin name on record in early colonial history he is considered the founding father of the name on the American continent. This same list of names is found in George Cabell Greer's book entitled "Early Virginia Immigrants (1622-1666). Also listed is a Robert Laughton possibly a brother to Leonard Laughton whose passage was arranged by William Wilkerson of New Norfolk, Virginia. This seems logical since brothers or close kin usually followed each other from the continent to early America. The two negroes without names were probably picked up when the ship passed by the Barbados Islands.

Most coming over were under some form of contractual agreement (indentured) whereby they agreed to work out the cost of their passage on plantations owned by rich proprietors in England many of whom never set foot in the colonies. These wealthy owners received tracts of land from kings and or royalty. Some early settlers were wealthy enough to pay their way however most were emigrants from the British Isles too poor to finance the voyage. To facilitate the immigration of such people Virginia offered "head rights" land grants of fifty acres for each new laborer. The person financing the laborer's voyage received not only the land grant but also the laborer's services for a period of years. Those under indentured contracts ranging from four to seven years pursuant to the conditions and terms of the contract however some completed their obligation sooner than others.

Not all "servants" came of their own free will. Some were forced into coming including prisoners from the crowded prisons in England. The government also transported prisoners taken in battles with the Scots and Irish in the 1650's to work on plantations in the new land. This was a dumping ground for undesirables including orphans, vagrants, paupers, and habitual criminal types. However most of the "servants" came willingly, eagerly attracted by the call and appeal of this new wilderness.

I am not sure of the terms of the contract for Leonard Laughton however land records in James City show within two years following his arrival he sold to a Seth Ward fifty acres of land in January 1639. I am not certain how he came into ownership of this acreage unless he came over under a special agreement with Elizabeth Sharpe whereby he would receive fifty acres for managing her farmlands in Henrico County. Perhaps he married the widow Sharpe. We discover in later records he was married to a woman named Elizabeth however about every other English woman was named Elizabeth out of regard for Queen Elizabeth during this period.

I mentioned previously receiving information from the archives in Jackson, Mississippi including a copy of the federal census of 1850 of Jasper County, Mississippi showing the household of Ezekiel A. Loftin and wife Elizabeth were six sons, the youngest my grandfather Leonard Lee Loftin born in 1849. Through this document I met my great grandfather for the first time. Included in the info from Jackson, Mississippi was a copy of the marriage license for my Loftin grandparents received in Jasper County. And of equal importance was a copy of A Genealogy of Loftin and Allied Families by the W. M. Creaseys (1936) of North Carolina.

Every genealogist I corresponded with tracing their Loftin ancestors eventually go through Leonard (1654) who settled in North Carolina circa 1688. The Creasys along with other genealogists show Leonard Loftin came from Pennsylvania which is true however at the time of his birth the territory in which his family lived was still part of the Virginia Colony. However by the time his oldest son Leonard (1654) settled in North Carolina in 1688 the above territory was part of the Pennsylvania Colony.

I was at first confused with the numerous derivatives of the Loftin name such as Laughton and Loughton however through correspondence with Doctor J. Lofting in Norwich, England I discovered the name had undergone several changes among those: Lofting, Loftings, Loftingh, Loftin, and Laughton. Dr. Lofting's primary interest in searching his ancestral lineage was to determine if tumors and deafness appearing in the family lineage were hereditary in origin. We both believed we are descended from a family who fled during a religious persecution to Holland where the family married into Dutch blood. Descendants of this family eventually returned to England and through time underwent several name changes mentioned previously. Often name changes occurred while a census was being made among illiterate people unable to write or spell their own names. In such instances the census taker wrote the name as it sounded to him.

Why did Leonard Laughton leave Henrico Province? I believe three conditions or situations motivated him to relocate. The first and perhaps foremost cause was economic. As a small tobacco grower he could not compete with the larger tobacco growers and planters in that province. Major growers in the area had thousands of acres under cultivation compared to the 500 acres or less owned by Leonard and Elizabeth. They had no wealthy businessmen in London backing them when a crop failed as did the larger growers most of whom had received their property from befriending the monarch in England.

The region between the York and James River was owned by large growers most of whom never set foot in the province and appointed overseers to farm the land. Since there were no regulations controlling subsidies or monopolies small business people were unable to compete with their larger competitors. The smallest growers sold out to the bigger owners who generously allowed them to continue working their farms for a share of the profits. I believe Leonard Laughton was too proud to place himself in bondage opting instead to search for a place where he would not be obligated to anyone. This trait of independence was passed down through generations of his descendants.

A second reason for the move was the harsh discipline and regulations of the Anglican Church by proprietors administering the affairs of the colony. Refusal to attend church was one of several acts resulting in severe discipline including public floggings and reprimands in front of family and friends. Drinking or use of tobacco or gambling as well as profanity led to severe punishment. This atmosphere resulted in an atmosphere of fear and caused neighbors to spy on their neighbors reporting any slight misdemeanor.

How ironic these early settlers to the colony came in order to practice their faith without fear of persecution only to find harsher penalties imposed on their movements in the colony. These conditions led many including Leonard and Elizabeth to seek another territory where they could practice their faith in relative freedom from persecution. Such a colony or territory came was Maryland carved out of Virginia territory around the Chesapeake Bay. A colony was established in this area where Catholics and others could practice their faith without fear of reprisals however the proprietors of the Maryland Colony eventually had another problem on their hands. Protestants came in such numbers they were soon were in positions of authority. Once in control they established rules restricting Roman Catholics to practice their religion. No priest could hold mass publicly and offer the sacraments. How ironic!!

Catholics soon found themselves worse off than they were in England under Elizabeth however they persevered. Since there were no catholic schools or seminaries allowed in the colony some sent their children back to France to receive training under the Jesuit's the great teachers of the faith. They were highly intelligent citizens and determined to gain the respect of their fellow countrymen and contribute to the growth of their colony and country. Time would see a change in these regulations and Catholic landowners would eventually be elected to positions of authority within their colonial legislative councils.

A third possible cause for Leonard Laughton leaving Henrico was fear of another uprising by Indians angry at the encroachment of colonists forcing them from land their ancestors had occupied for centuries. The aggressive behavior by colonists would continue without ceasing resulting in tribes being deprived of their land and being killed or placed on reservations. The white man had little consideration for the claims of the Indians who occupied this continent for over 10,000 years prior to the arrival of the first white men.

Powhattan chief of the Indian Confederacy at first befriended the early settlers and assisted them through the terrible times of starvation and deprivation in 1606-1609 however upon his death he was succeeded by an older brother, Opechancanough who harbored a deep hatred for the intruders and in 1622 led an uprising resulting in the massacre of three hundred men, women, and children. Tempers may have cooled, however, I believe Leonard Laughton sensed another uprising was near, left the Henrico Province in Virginia, and relocated to the Shenandoah River Valley near the mouth of Chesapeake Bay.

This area would eventually become the colony of Pennsylvania where people could worship without fear of persecution. It was here he and wife raised a family including four sons whose descendants later would be found over most of the states of the union. We are not sure the oldest son's name is however there is information which indicates his name was John. The name appeared on a will probated of Jane King stating she had two sons one named John Loftin the other Robert King leading to the assumption her first marriage was to a John Loftin her second to Robert King. She appointed John Mills executor of her will giving custody of her minor sons to this individual.

Cornelius married and had a family including a son named Cornelius Jr who along with his father purchased land in James city, Virginia? William married and settled in an area now where the city of Baltimore is located. He lived there in 1697, 1698 and 1699. Leonard (1654) my ancestor carried the name to North Carolina in 1688 where he and his wife produced a family of seven children including three sons whom we will meet in the following chapter.

Prior to continuation of tracing the footsteps of

Leonard Loftin (1654) to North Carolina we offer some opinions concerning the character and nature of the man alleged to be the Founding Father of the name in America. Obviously he was a man of courage with confidence in his ability to make a living for himself and his family there in the quiet confines of the Susquehanna River Valley. He could have sold out placing himself in bondage to some large owner however the desire for freedom drove him onward searching for the place where he could make a new life for himself and his family.

What kind of background did he come from? We cannot be certain of his status at the time he came to America apparently not from any privileged family or he could have paid his passage to the colonies. He chose the wilderness leaving the strict regulations and laws of the Virginia Colony to enter a country where few white men had ever set foot to live by his wits and what he couldn't take with the hoe, plow or gun he did without.

There is little else I can add about this first Loftin on American soil. I do not know why he came only thankful he came. If he had chosen to remain on English soil I would not be sitting here attempting to write this story of my Loftin family in America. He went to his grave without realizing his descendants would eventually spread over the entire American continent. In the following chapters we trace the footsteps of one branch of his family tree through North Carolina, South Carolina, Georgia, Mississippi and eventually to Texas.

Chapter Two
*The Trail from Pennsylvania
to North Carolina
Leonard Loftin*
1654-1721*

We have a considerable amount of information on Leonard Loftin (1654) who settled near Albemarle Sound in North Carolina in 1688. Why he settled in such a miserable area of swamps, marshes, lowlands and creeks is beyond me. Conditions must have been bad in Pennsylvania for him to relocate to this area however proprietors were offering large tracts of land to anyone willing to live on the land for a certain period of time. Evidently Leonard was satisfied as he remained in this area of the colony the remainder of his life. He and wife Elizabeth raised six children their names shown in a copy of his will on file in the archives of Raleigh, North Carolina. Leonard became prominent in the politics of his county and acquired considerable acreage on both the north and south shores of Albemarle Sound.

This property on Albemarle Bay with access to the Atlantic through time passed into hands of commercial developers who sold it to the federal government. During WW II the government built a large Marine Training Bases in this area. While tracking my ancestors it became obvious several of them had difficulty holding onto property which eventually became extremely valuable. However some of Leonard's children held onto property they inherited in this area which passed down and is still owned by descendants of Leonard and son Benoni Loftin.

The North Carolina colony where Leonard and family lived was later divided into North and South Carolina. The argument continues to this day which got the better deal. South Carolinians argue they did since they inherited Charleston one of the largest seaports in the world along fine farmlands and a thriving fishing industry.

Leonard and sons, Cornelius, Leonard and Benoni contributed to the early development of the North Carolina Colony and their accomplishments are recorded on the land records as well as those of Saint Paul's Anglican Church in Edenton. Leonard Loftin served as warden in the church from 1712 through 1714 and on the vestry of the church from 1715 through 1717. He served on the General Council of Chowan Province responsible for settling disputes concerning land issues and criminal cases. He also was commissioner of roads and controller of accounts at one time or other. Obviously a man of some importance dedicated to his immediate province as well as state. His sons to some degree followed in his footsteps. The outstanding service to community and state by this man and his sons led to the family being included among the fifteen most prominent families in North Carolina during the period from 1712 through 1785.

Elizabeth Loftin his wife died circa 1715 about the time Leonard sold his acreage on the south shore of Albemarle Sound and moved to Craven County where he died in 1721. In his will he was quite specific concerning how his property was to be dispersed among members of his family. He charged Cornelius and Leonard with the care of Benoni, and their three sisters until they were old enough to care for themselves. They were to build a home for Benoni near Kingston or if not then purchase a place for him to live and tend his stock until he was of age. The name Benoni captured my attention basically because it seemed not of English origin and simply because it was not passed along to future generations of this lineage. I believe it represents the merger of two names shortened into one.

From reviewing his last will and testament it seems obvious Leonard taught his sons to assume responsibility toward their community, church and state as well as their obligation to neighbors. We tend to forget the mother of these children also had a definite role in their upbringing unfortunately in genealogy little attention is given to the maternal branch of the family albeit of equal importance.

In an effort to discover more about Leonard Loftin's life in the Edenton area I wrote to the Rector of Saint Paul's Church in Edenton, N.C. hoping their records would reveal additional information concerning his family. Elizabeth Moore church secretary responded to my letter with the following information.

Leonard Loftin may have first settled in Chowan but proveth rights for himself and wife Elizabeth in 1694 in Perquimans Precinct. In 1697 he was one of the overseers of the highways in this precinct. His son Leonard was born in Perquimans January 15, 1698. In 1701 he bought land in Chowan Precinct apparently south of Albemarle Sound on what came to be called south shore or South Lancaster and he described himself as "of Chowan" in 1705. Mary Loftin his youngest daughter died in Perquimans in1707.

Leonard was a justice by the spring of 1711, in a 1714 power of attorney he was called Captain Loftin and his son Cornelius was old enough to sign as a witness. He possibly had financial difficulties in 1715 for in April of that year he sold his home plantation to Colonel Thomas Bullock and assigned a 1712 patent to Jacob Blount. No explanation of what kind of patent this was. Colonel Bullock's will identified one tract of land as being "where Leonard Loftin lives" referring to the son of Leonard Loftin who continued living on the south shore two months after the proving of his father's will. She also described the name of the first daughter of Leonard as Priscilla not Dorcellay.

Cornelius Loftin oldest son was a justice in 1733 in Craven County and amassed considerable land in addition to the farm his father had given him. His descendants remained along the eastern coast of our nation. Leonard the second oldest son inherited the home plantation in Craven and through the years acquired additional property along Hancock Creek. He married Sarah Martin daughter of Thomas and Elizabeth Martin of South River, Craven County both mentioned in their wills. Mrs. Martin also referred to ten grandchildren in her will however none of them were Loftin grandchildren.

In regard to burial sites of Leonard and Elizabeth the church records of Saint Paul's Church in Edenton did not contain such data that far back. Saint Paul's parish covered a broad area and vestrymen living in certain areas of the parish forwarded birth, marriage, death records to the main church at Edenton however record keeping wasn't well documented at that time and consequently lost to posterity.

Traveling ministers usually spent a week or so preaching and conducting services in such remote areas. Each landowner usually designated burial sites on their own property since it wasn't practical to move a body any long distance as preservation techniques had not been perfected. In some rare instances family descendants have maintained records of their ancestor's burial plots and maintained these plots however given time nature obliterates all traces of graves. Families occasionally had relatives residing in their homes that died and were buried on the property further confusing future genealogists and historians.

This is all I can offer regarding Leonard Loftin 1654 who with wife and a young family left Pennsylvania to relocate to the lowlands of North Carolina. Like his father he must have been a man of conviction and courage to cope with the challenges confronting the early settlers. Like so many others they expanded the boundaries of the developing colonies on the American continent. Leonard left three sons to carry on his legacy the youngest Benoni was my ancestor.

BENONI LOFTIN*
(1705-1756) North Carolina

Benoni Loftin much loved by his father apparently became a person of some influence in North Carolina however I was unable to locate a great deal of information about him especially following the passing of his parents. Most of the information I include in this history about Benoni is taken from the will of his father.

He was born January 15, 1705 and died January 6, 1756 fifty-six years later. There are some records in Craven County proving he established himself as one of the major property owners and business leaders in the Craven Precinct. According to their father's last wishes his older brothers had a home built for their younger brother near Kingston, North Carolina, which was still standing at the time of the writing of the genealogy by the Creasys in 1936.

The home place of Benoni Loftin named Jericho was still standing when I began working on this history at the beginning of the 1990's. Robert Dunn and the estate of Francis Clyde Dunn all descendants of Benoni were owners of this property in 1936. The property remains today in the possession of descendants of his we were told. When the old place had to be torn down another home was built across the branch which later passed into the hands of Walter Dunn, Jr who married Cynthia Loftin a great granddaughter of Benoni.

According to the Creasy's genealogy Mrs. W.M. (Gertrude Bagby) Creasy was born in this house built in 1756 by Elkhannah Loftin son of Benoni Loftin. (This explains the Creasy's genealogy research resulting in their Genealogy of Loftin and Allied Families back in 1936. Their findings were published and now on record in the State Archives of North Carolina. (N.C. State Colonial Records, Volume XXII, p. 324, Jan 6, 1751. This gives Colonial Dames Eligibility). I found no information regarding Benoni Loftin's first wife and there appears to be agreement Susannah Burtonshall, his second wife, was the mother of his children.

Thomas
Elkhannah
Elizabeth
John
Leonard
Frederick
Francis
Samuel
Ezekiel

Records show Benoni Loftin served on the General Assembly and filled the position of Tax Assessor while serving with the Craven Precinct Militia preceding the outbreak of war with the mother country. He was around 16 years of age when his father died however well taken care of in his father's last will and testament. I find little information of his life except that shown previously in the Creasy's genealogy. Leonard and Cornelius his brothers apparently carried out their father's wishes regarding Benoni and their young sisters. It would be interesting to know what happened in the dispensing of the estate among his sisters.

Benoni evidently came into possession of property and managed it well since records indicate since it remained in the hands of his descendants (Creaseys) at least through 1936. Without any facts or credible information such as wills and land transactions we can only surmise as to the internal affairs of this ancestor and dispensation of any property. The Creasys describe his property and home where he lived out his life and refer to it as Jericho. I include the following since a brother of mine in later years after reading this history also named his home place by that name.

First names are often passed from generation to generation. Leonard Harmon Loftin my oldest brother was given the first name of his father, Leonard Harrison Loftin and Leonard Lee Loftin his grandfather. This brother of mine, fascinated with the early history of our ancestors, placed a large sign at the entrance to his property northwest of Sour Lake, Texas bearing the name Jericho. His one room house set in the southern fringes of the Big Thicket near the town of Sour Lake in southeast Texas.

There in the woods around Jericho he lived with his blue tick, black and tan hounds and a multitude of chickens and guineas. He lived well off squirrels, deer and wild hogs. Guineas roosting in the trees around the house served as watchdogs against intruders. His.12 gauge pump shotgun loaded with Number 2 buckshot was always near his bed. He loved the lonesome however he managed early morning runs to Sour Lake where he had breakfast and spent time in swapping stories with old timers mostly retired from oil companies which flourished during the boom days in the area.

He loved his life style free of little responsibility but was well loved and thought of within his community and the county as a whole. Probably more so than anyone he was delighted to discover through the pages of The Loftin Chronicles our ancestral lineage back to the founding father. Showed the book to each and every one he knew. Those with a sense of history seem to more deeply appreciate some knowledge of where they came from especially those forming a link in their ancestral chain. So it was with not only my brother but the remainder of my family.

By way of reflection, it appears obvious the important legacy of Benoni Loftin was eight sons whose descendants spread the Loftin name over our country. Ezekiel the youngest my ancestor was quite an interesting individual who led a remarkably complex life so much so I refer to him as The Maverick. His choice of allegiance during the Revolutionary War concerned me at first. In the following chapter is information indicating Ezekiel served with the British during the Revolutionary War.

EZEKIEL LOFTIN*
(THE MAVERICK)
(1750-1835) North Carolina

This ancestor proved to be a most intriguing personage one not hesitant to go against the flow of popular opinion and align himself with unpopular issues of his time. Such an attitude brought great hardship to him and his loved ones even to the point of being ostracized by family and friends forcing him to seek refuge far removed from his home place in Dobbs County (Lenoir) North Carolina. Let's take a look at this maverick and try to determine what made him tick!

Ezekiel Loftin born August 17, 1750 in Dobbs (Lenoir) County, North Carolina was around six years of age when his father died. Benoni's second wife, Susannah Burtonshall, had died or was incapable of caring for Ezekiel so the court apparently placed him in the care of one an older brother (Leonard or Cornelius). There is scarcity of information describing his early years only the times were known to be most troubling as tension increased between the colonies and England.

Rebellious colonial representatives began speaking out against the injustices imposed on them by King George in England. Patrick Henry among the most eloquent of these speakers could inflame an audience within minutes and did so with speeches ending with such phrases as "Throw off these chains of slavery liberty! Give me liberty or give me death! "He was not alone as there was increasing resentment throughout the colonies against the king and his parliament over unfair taxes levied on the colonies without them having representation in Parliament. "Taxation without representation" went the cry across the broad Atlantic to the ears of the king and his lawmakers who shrugged their shoulders and ignored such pleas. Time would prove they should have listened more seriously to what they perceived as only complaints against their monarch and his rightful duty to regulate as he so chose.

In 1775 the representatives of the colonies gathered in Philadelphia and forged a document declaring their separation from England and establishing a system of government for themselves. Some colonists who dearly loved their mother country felt this was going too far and sought to restrain their fiery brothers asking instead for representation in the English Parliament where they could petition the king for a redress of grievances.

I came upon information indicating Ezekiel Loftin's brothers served in the military of the colonies during the Revolutionary War while Ezekiel remained loyal to Great Britain. Ezekiel and two neighbors from Craven County, Aaron Lambert and William Russell served in the same company under Colonel Cox also from Craven County and received wounds which placed them in his Majesty's Hospital in August 1781. Mrs. Sophie Martin whose collateral ancestor was Aaron Lambert has done extensive research of the records of Craven County-deeds and came across data showing these three men and Cox were neighbors and several intermarriages among their families.

Mrs. Martin was certain Ezekiel Lofton shown on the stoppages at the Wilmington Hospital was the son of Benoni and brother of Thomas her ancestor. Two of Thomas daughters married two younger brothers of Aaron Lambert. The information described by Mrs. Martin concerning these three men being hospitalized at the Wilmington Hospital in August 1781 is also in Robert O. Demond's book entitled The Loyalists in North Carolina during the Revolution. This information seemingly confirms my ancestor Ezekiel Loftin wasn't one of those super patriots on the order of Patrick Henry or James Otis.

I was somewhat disappointed to discover this about my ancestor however after studying those times I wondered what I would have done if faced with the same situation? Easy to sit here and be judgmental far removed from those times knowing the revolution led to the most successful form of democratic government the world has ever seen. Easy to forget at that critical point in history these people were first generation English with deep ties to their ancestral roots. Would I have chosen to oppose the mother country? Not an easy choice to make. Perhaps we should pause to reconsider our country's early beginning.

It has been circa two hundred thirty-six years since that first shot was aimed at British soldiers at Yorktown. The entire East Coast was aflame with possible revolt from the Crown. It's interesting to read of those days in the colonies when so many radical ideas were being discussed among thinking men and women.

We know about the forerunners, the leaders, of our bid for independence from England, George Washington, Alexander Hamilton, John Adams, and Benjamin Franklin. One would wonder why such wealthy landed men would have rebelled. A revolution usually is led by the disenfranchised, those who have nothing to lose by making a stand against tyranny.

But America's patriots, the rich as well as those of ordinary means knew full well what they were up against when they put their signatures to the Declaration of Independence in 1776. King George was an unforgiving absolute monarch who wouldn't hesitate to strip them of their property and hand it over to Loyalists. Those were desperate days!

As it reads at the end of the Declaration of Independence:" we mutually pledge to each other our Lives, our Fortunes, and our sacred honor." It was no hollow promise.

From all the Colonies, fifty-six men signed the document. The signers sensed that terrible times lay ahead as a result of their names on that fateful document. Some would manage to escape complete confiscation but there were others who had homes burned and lost all their land and wealth. John Hancock scrawled his name in large bold letters indicating he wanted to bring it to the attention of King George.

That revolution can also be considered a civil war. Families were torn apart when it came to declaring their loyalties and few felt comfortable sitting on the fence.

Washington's friend and neighbor, George William Fairfax, sailed for England and never returned. Many Loyalists, called Tories packed up and migrated north; their descendants can be found there today. Franklin's son William, had received a lucrative appointment from the Crown, told his father that he could not in good conscience turn his back on the King. Serving as governor of New Jersey, he ended up as one of the leaders of the Loyalists. Bitter quarrels ensued and finally William moved his family to England. Years later they reconciled. This may present for the reader some understanding of the divided loyalties within the colonies during this revolution. It was helpful to me understanding Ezekiel Loftin's position during the conflict.

There is a copy of an application for pension Ezekiel Loftin age 82 filed with the War Department in Washington, D. C. while living in Lawrence County, Mississippi. I secured a copy of this application containing the following information in support of his claim: Born August 17, 1750 in Dobbs County, North Carolina/While a resident of Dobbs County in 1771 served as a minute man for one month under Captain Jesse Cobb then served three years as a mechanic under Quartermaster General John Tillery at Kingston, North Carolina. After the war he lived two years in North Carolina, two years in South Carolina, and about seventeen years in Georgia thence on to Mississippi. His claim was not allowed, as he did not serve six months in a military capacity during the Revolution as required by the pension law.

This data was taken from a copy of a letter Commissioner Winfield Scott of the War Department

Pension Office sent to Mrs. Seaburg, Temple, Texas who had initiated an inquiry concerning Ezekiel Loftin. General Scott reply to Mrs. Seaburg is basically the same information Ezekiel shows on his application for pension to the War Department. There was no mention in the correspondence from the War Department Ezekiel Loftin was a British sympathizer. Another puzzling aspect of this situation is why Ezekiel would submit an application for a pension to the government he allegedly fought against! Coming across this document concerning an ancestor who allegedly fought against his own kinsmen in this Revolutionary War was hard to understand. After sorting through all of the information which surfaced concerning Ezekiel I still remain uncertain as to where his allegiance was during the Revolutionary War.

In search for a logical explanation as to his behavior, I read countless documents and never came away completely satisfied as to his motivation and loyalty to the crown. He joined with others in opposing unfair taxation imposed by King George and insisted on representation in Parliament but chose to plead the cause before resorting to rebellion. When all was said and done they could not support a declaration of independence separating them from their mother country. This action proved costly for Tories who were ostracized after the war resulting in many fleeing from North Carolina to South Carolina with the intention of boarding English ships to leave the country or leave in search of a new beginning further inland. What information I have leads me to believe Ezekiel was among those finding life unbearable after the conflict and decided to move with his wife, Charlotte, and son,

Asa, where they could make a new beginning. I am glad he decided to stay rather than board a ship for England. How I came upon the information showing Ezekiel was twice married producing two families was a matter of luck and or divine providence!

ASA LOFTIN*
(1784) North Carolina

Information regarding two marriages of Ezekiel was brought to my attention by Margaret Johnson of Palacios, Texas. (My initial research showed Ezekiel marrying a Jennie Linder in Georgia during his movement through that state.) Mrs. Johnson suggested I was missing a generation and advised me to contact Arnold Johnson of Rosepine, Louisiana also researching this Loftin lineage. I contacted Arnold who forwarded records showing Ezekiel Loftin 1750 NC married twice His first wife was Charlotte, who bore them a son named Asa (1784) NC. This was news to me. Until this time the only information I had was Ezekiel's marriage to Jennie Linder, mother of five children: Ezekiel Jr. 1792, John 1794, Adah 1797, Giles T. 1799, and Elizabeth circa 1804. How Loftin came into possession of the family records of Asa Loftin is worth repeating.

Asa Loftin fathered fifteen children four with Faney Consas his first wife and eleven with Rachel Haggar his second wife. Fortunately for those of us who began searching for our Loftin roots Asa recorded the names of his children in his family bible which was preserved and passed down to his youngest child Sinthia. Sinthia married a man name Moses who was killed in the Civil War and then she later married Issac Hall who informed Arnold Loftin his grandmother was a descendant of Asa Loftin. Copies of his family records were in the possession of Hazel Howell, a great grandchild of Sinthia Moses Hall, living in Pineville, Louisiana. Arnold contacted Mrs. Howell who graciously provided a copy of Asa Loftin's family records containing names and birthdates of his children. It was through Arnold Loftin I discovered Asa Loftin was my great grandfather. Interestingly enough Asa is also Arnold Loftin's great grandfather. I descend from Asa's marriage to Faney Consas while Arnold descends from Asa's marriage to Rachel Haggar.

Now we continue the trail of our ancestors, Ezekiel and son Asa and their families through South Carolina, Georgia, and eventually to Lawrence County, Mississippi.

Chapter Three
South Carolina/Georgia/Mississippi

We can only imagine the troubles and problems confronting families following the end of the American Revolution. Especially with families of divided allegiance who came home from the conflict. I am not certain how long Ezekiel Loftin, Charlotte and Asa lived in South Carolina before moving to Georgia however a good estimate would be about two or three years. The family was in Richmond County, Georgia in the early 1790's as records show Ezekiel received a land grant of 200 acres in that county in 1795. Other records show he took part in a land lottery in Washington Co.in1800 while Asa his son also participated in a land lottery in Wilkinson Co., Ga. in 1807.

Soon after the family arrived in Georgia, Charlotte has disappeared from the family record and Ezekiel marries Jennie Linder in 1792. Linder is Scotch, and we found the name on records of Lawrence County, Mississippi where this couple will later move. The family of Ezekiel and Jennie Linder is shown as follows:

*Ezekiel Jr. 2 March 1792
John (1794)
Giles (1796)

Adah (1798)
Elizabeth (1804)

I hesitate to deviate from my line of descent through Asa at this point to include the family of Ezekiel Jr. however it is important to understand the confusion created by the two marriages of Ezekiel Loftin 1750 followed later by two marriages of Asa Loftin, his son. The first names of several in these family circles are identical passed along from generation to generation lending to confusion by those later searching for these ancestors.

Ezekiel Loftin, Jr. married Jane Allen in Georgia 1811 and their children are as follows:

Sabina Jane Loftin, born 1 March 1814
Society (Sciota) Loftin, born 19 April 1816
Martin Elias Loftin, born 20 August 1818
Giles Thomas Loftin, born 7 December 1820
Leonard Lee Loftin, born 10, February 1823 (Same name as my grandfather 1849)
William West Loftin, born 6 July 1825
Minerva Loftin, born 1828
James Riley Loftin, born 10 March 1831
Eli Harvey Loftin, born 17 September 1833
Willis Turner Loftin, born 18 August 1836

I include this family to show how certain names such as Ezekiel, Giles, Thomas, and Leonard are passed down from generation to generation on both paternal and maternal sides of family.

Don H. Loftin

ASA AND FANEY CONSAS FAMILY

Now we introduce the family of Asa Loftin who around the age of nineteen marries Faney Consas December 1, 1803 probably in Richmond County, Georgia. Their children are as follows:

Ezekiel Andrew* December 25, 1804
John, Ezekiel's twin brother
James February 7, 1807
Major February 12, 1812

Major was not a member of this family but a kinsman visiting Asa's family at the time of the census.

I found little information about my great grandfather Ezekiel Andrew Loftin while in Georgia. Faney Consas his mother apparently died circa 1812-1814 as she disappears from the family records. Asa, a widower, moved Ezekiel Andrew and his brothers John and James to Lawrence County where their father Ezekiel (1750) and wife Jennie Linder had previously moved.

Ezekiel Andrew Loftin was around twelve years of age when the family moved to Lawrence County. I am not certain what happened to John the twin brother of Ezekiel Andrew Loftin my great grandfather? I have had numerous requests from other genealogists over the years wanting information about this twin brother to my great grandfather. The only information I have regards a John Loftin and wife buried in Rocky Hill Cemetery in Alabama circa age my Ezekiel Andrew Loftin.

LAWRENCE COUNTY

Records of Lawrence County, Mississippi, show Ezekiel Andrew Loftin lived there for a number of years before moving with his father Asa and wife and their new family to Neshoba County where Asa was overseer of a plantation. I find little else about Ezekiel A. Loftin until he marries a South Carolina girl Elizabeth Dyess in Jasper County, Mississippi. These great great grandparents of mine settled near Stringer in Jasper County where they raised several sons including my grandfather Leonard Lee.

As stated earlier, Ezekiel the Maverick settled near Oakvale in Lawrence County upon moving from Georgia. Here he lived out his life however some of his descendants can still be found in this area of Mississippi. In regards to finding the old home place of Ezekiel I accomplished little however through correspondence with Arnold Loftin of Rosepine, La. and a sister of a Giles Loftin Mrs. Lizzette Loftin Rawls of Hattiesburg, Mississippi proved helpful.

Arnold Loftin described a trip he and his son John made one Sunday afternoon to Lawrence County, Mississippi during the late 1970's in search of the old Loftin home place. Several persons talked with around Oakvale vaguely recalled an old Loftin home place located off Highway 13 between Prentiss and Columbia not far from the Greens Creek Baptist Church. They found the church and talked to a colored lady who gave them directions to an old homestead she thought once owned by an Allen Loftin now occupied by a Giles Loftin an employee of the State Highway Department. They found the house in question but no one there however a neighbor told them it was the home of Giles Loftin and yes he was an employee of the State Highway Department. They waited until dark set in and when no one showed up they headed back to Baton Rouge where his son lived. The neighbor did note Giles received his mail through the Oakvale Post Office.

I wrote to Giles Loftin, Rural Delivery, and Oakvale, explaining my interest in tracking down my Loftin ancestors listing Benoni 1705, Ezekiel 1750, Asa 1784, Ezekiel 1804, and Leonard Lee 1849.The response to my letter was from Lizette Loftin Rawls of Hattiesburg, Mississippi sister of Giles Loftin saying her brother had asked her to respond since he was in such poor health. It was a real informative letter.

Their father Allen Loftin married Jane Polk and raised ten children there in Lawrence County, Mississippi. They are certain their father is a descendant of Ezekiel Loftin Jr who married Jane Allen who settled in Oakvale, Mississippi where they raised ten children. The family list forwarded by Mrs. Rawls is identical to the one included earlier. Her brother Giles could recall the names of Giles, Leonard, Martin and Minerva among the ten children. This information proves Ezekiel Loftin, Jr. and Asa Loftin are half-brothers. This was the last contact I had with Mrs. Rawls or brother Giles. At this point, let's take a closer look at the family from the marriage of Asa and Rachel. Seems there were eleven children born to this couple.

ASA AND RACHEL LOFTIN'S FAMILY

Asa and Rachel Hagar were married July 23, 1818 in Lawrence County Mississippi. Their children, born in Lawrence County, are as follows:

Born in Lawrence County, Mississippi

Asa Loftin Jr	January 11, 1819
Benagh Loftin	September 23, 1820
Mary Loftin	December 8, 1822
Anna Loftin	December 5, 1824
Rachel Loftin	May 6, 1827
Fanaty Loftin	April 26, 1829
Delilia Loftin	May 5, 1832
Marcus T. Loftin	December 18, 1834
Avaline Loftin	April 1, 1837

Born in Lauderdale County, Mississippi

Amaline Loftin	June 17, 1838
Sinthia Loftin	March 14, 1843

The youngest child of Asa and Rachel proved a vital link pin in continuing the bridge of genealogy that brought Arnold Loftin of Deridder, La. and this author together during our search for ancestors in the 1980's. Our correspondence eventually led to our meeting in October 1987.

Leonard Harmon Loftin, my oldest brother, and I drove to Rosepine, Louisiana and spent the day with Arnold. He was outside his home surrounded by large oaks and pines waiting for our arrival. What a pleasure to finally meet this man who had shared so generously critical information regarding our common lineage.

After introductions and meeting with his son and wife, we began discussion our backgrounds and family history. What a fine time we had comparing and sharing data.

My brother, never one to meet strangers, quickly joined our discussion contributing interesting information about our Loftin kinsmen who lived in Hardin and Trinity County. This information intrigued Arnold since he had kinsmen who had settled around Crockett and before long they were on common ground laughing and talking about kinsmen in northeastern Texas. Harmon surely knew about every person or so it seemed living in northeast Texas as well as several across the way in Louisiana. Their conversation became so animated I had difficulty in getting them back to the purpose of our visit that being examining our ancestral lineage as far back as possible.

During the discussion, Arnold presented information about Asa moving to Lauderdale County where he was an overseer on a cotton plantation. Later, Asa moved to Neshoba County where he is reported to have died around 1860. Arnold Loftin recalled his grandfather William N. Loftin saying he remembered his father Benagh mentioning only three members of the family he grew up with: Markus T. C., Sinthia, and Zeke, who surely was my great grandfather Ezekiel Andrew.

They once lived close to each other in Jasper County, Mississippi. Benagh and wife Sina Stennett lived in Sylverena eight miles north of Ezekiel's home near Stringer. He was a blacksmith and gunsmith by trade while Zeke and his family were farmers. Benagh and wife Sina had several children and when Asa Loftin died in 1860 they took Sinthia and Markus T.C., into their home.

Murdock one of Benagh's sons was in the Confederate Army during the siege of Vicksburg and captured but released after the war ended. Sinthia married a man named Moses who was killed during the Civil War. She married again this time to a man named Hall and settled in Beauregard Parish Louisiana. Her brother Markus T C also moved to this area and had several children some of whom crossed the Sabine to settle in Trinity County. Benagh moved from Jasper County circa 1868 to Louisiana and settled on Bundicks Creek seven miles southeast of present day DeRidder. He passed away in the home of his son William N Loftin in 1895 in Evans; Louisiana. William N. Loftin's son, Murph Loftin operated a ferry on the Sabine River the boundary line between Texas and Louisiana. All of this info concerning Benagh, Sinthia and Markus T C settling in Louisiana was important when I began tracing the movement of my Loftin ancestors from Jasper County Mississippi to Hardin County Texas.

When we left Arnold Loftin's home place that October day in 1987 I sensed this was the last time we would see each other and so it was. Prior to our departure he showed us his grape vineyard. We then walked back to the front where we said our goodbyes. He was standing waving as we drove out of sight. We continued corresponding frequently until around the end of the 1990's when the letters stopped coming. I thank God for allowing our paths to cross for a very special moment in time. God moves in mysterious ways His wonders to behold!

Chapter Four
The Move to Texas

In this chapter I retrace the movement of the wagon train which brought my Loftin ancestors from Jasper County, Mississippi to the county of Hardin in southeast Texas and those who made the trip. Logic dictates it was during the spring of 1873 when the oxen drawn wagons pulled away from the old home stead of my Great Grandfather Ezekiel Andrew Loftin near Stringer, Mississippi and headed for the Big Thicket in Hardin County, Texas.

My father said his parents Leonard Lee and Frances Collins Loftin, along with his grandmother, Elizabeth Dyess Loftin, and several of his uncles and their families came on nine wagons drawn by oxen. Most families migration to Texas during this period of time used wagons or two wheel carts each pulled by a yoke of oxen.

Several of Frances Collin's kinsmen made the trip. After reaching Hardin County some of the Collins continued on to northeast Texas settling in Trinity and Houston Counties. Elizabeth Loftin was a widow as Ezekiel A. Loftin died circa 1868-1870 and been laid to rest either on their farm or in a cemetery around Stringer.

The following information is my own description of the trip to Texas of these ancestors of mine.

Elizabeth circa 68 years old rode on one wagon with her youngest son James (19) while Albert (22) another son drove a team pulling a wagon loaded with their possessions and supplies. On the other wagons were Andrew (35), Ezekiel (33), Giles (28) Thomas (26), and Leonard Lee (21) with some of these having families of their own.

As of this writing I can only assume Giles Loftin (28) made the trip to Texas but if so he returned to Mississippi as there is no record of his settling in Hardin County or northeast Texas. Also Giles Loftin's descendants show up on records in Lawrence County around Oakvale, Mississippi. John Charles Loftin (30) third oldest son wasn't with the group. We have credible information showing he deserted from the Confederate Army during the battle of Vicksburg headed for Indian Territory (Oklahoma). He reappears later searching for mother and brothers who had settled in Hardin County.

Those who chance to read this should understand the circumstances that caused the Loftins and neighbors to leave Mississippi and move to Texas. The Civil War left most families in the south destitute and history shows those in charge of administrating the recovery were vindictive in their treatment of the defeated southerners. Lincoln, prior to his assassination, emphatically warned the post reconstruction era would be administered with compassion and understanding. He insisted the south assume their rightful roles in government at the federal, state and local levels.

However, Abe Lincoln was not around to enforce his directives and those assigned the responsibility for reconstruction resorted in some situations to rubbing the noses of the southerners in the dirt and having them eat crow. Some administrators placed freed slaves in positions of authority, which was like rubbing salt in a wound. The Loftins were obviously poor but too proud to live under such regulations and conditions so they looked elsewhere to make a new start.

I am certain my grandmother Frances Collins Loftin was instrumental in convincing her husband's family to move to Hardin County. Frances Collins daughter of Simeon and Lydia Bynum Collins was born in Jones County. Her uncle, Stacy Collins with wife and three sons, Stacey Jr., Warren and Edward and their families moved to Hardin County Texas during the 1850's settling in The Big Thicket.

Stacey Artist planted crops and hunted the black bear, deer and squirrel in the dense forest. The Collins lived a peaceful existence free from the mores of society and restrictions of government. Through the years these Collins' relatives corresponded with Frances urging her and family to join them in the Thicket saying there's room for everyone.

This fell on deaf ears at first however as the depression continued and times worsened Ezekiel and neighbors became more distressed. These hard times probably contributed to the death of Ezekiel leaving his widow and sons to make decisions regarding their future. They were unable to pay taxes on their farms and faced foreclosures. I feel strongly Elizabeth was convinced by Frances Collins Loftin it was in the best interest of everyone to move to Hardin County, Texas where her Collins relatives were living. Within a year or so after the passing of Ezekiel Elizabeth, her sons decided to pack up and leave for Texas. Frances Loftin sent word to her kinsmen in Hardin County they were on their way. Data available lead me to believe the move occurred during the spring of 1873. (Other historians say 1872.)

The situation in Mississippi had to be unbearable for Elizabeth in her late sixties to relocate to southeast Texas. She surely had misgivings leaving the home where her sons were born and on land they farmed for over thirty years. So many memories! She surely understood there was little chance she would ever come this way again. And she was leaving behind the man she loved and stood by for over forty years. I believe she consented to the move wanting her sons and grandchildren to have a chance for better lives.

I am not aware of the extent or size of the families of her other sons however we know Leonard and Frances Collins Loftin had two children, Paula Jane (4) and Frances Amanda (2) at the time. There were other infants and youngsters among the other families. Conditions were surely bad for these families to even consider pulling up stakes and heading for a strange land.

The trip from Jasper County Mississippi to Hardin County took at least a month and a half however this is an estimate on my part. The terrain was brutal with major rivers compounding their route of travel. Some of the men rode horses others walked beside the wagons with women and small children inside. Milk cows and other livestock plodded behind the nine canvas covered wagons. Most of the wagons, we believe, were large two wheel carts.

The wagons were loaded with essential foodstuffs, i.e., flour, beans, bacon, dried fruit, and coffee; sugar, salt and vinegar. Plows, axes, bucksaws, rocking chairs, chamber pots, cast iron skillets, Dutch ovens, water kegs and butter churns were tied to the sides of the wagons. Some precious things were brought along i.e.; fiddles and harmonicas and guitars for music and singing. There were no books with exception of family bibles since most were illiterate.

The second day after leaving their home they arrived at the old Ezekiel Loftin place on Pearl River near Oakvale where they spent a few days with relatives. After leaving Oakvale they crossed the Mississippi River below Vicksburg by ferry boat into Louisiana. They moved in a southwesterly direction toward Benagh Loftin's home on Bundicks Creek near the sawmill town of Sugartown a few miles north of DeRidder.

The days became wearisome for man and beast. As the oxen strained heads down against the rattling chains and hickory yokes fighting to keep moving through mud axle deep in some areas. Occasionally the wheels became stuck requiring the aid of several men to free the wagon from the much. While the older ones suffered the younger considered this a great adventure running and playing around the train. Above the din an unattended axle shrieked crying for grease while in another wagon something fell with a crash awakening a sleeping infant who began crying. Such was a typical day on the trail of my ancestors to Texas.

The wagon train crossed several rivers on its way to Texas including the Mississippi and Sabine. All crossed by ferry which presented a problem since the livestock especially the horses were not too anxious to get aboard and float across a flowing river. Some days the weather was terrible with thunderstorms drenching everyone the wagons pulled into thick stands of timber seeking shelter for themselves and their animals. How they made such a trip without someone dying of pneumonia is a mystery however they kept moving believing there were better days lay ahead.

There are my assumptions about the trip, however, I'm certain there were dogs trotting beside the wagons. Each family had two or three canines they used for working their cattle and or for hunting. Possibly the most important asset of these animals was their loyalty and determination to protect their owners and their families and property. They considered the turf they lived on their own and they would rip the throat out of anyone or anything, which came uninvited on that property. Many a stranger found one of these curs at their throat if they walked unannounced through the front gate leading up to the house. The dogs usually slept in the dogtrot or underneath the front porch. They were stocky built cur dogs yellow in color with black mouths. The stocky build resulted from some previous generation inviting a bulldog to share his genealogy with this strain of animal.

I first discovered these dogs in the possession of early Loftin ancestors in North Carolina and Southern Pennsylvania. Ezekiel Loftin (1750) brought two of these animals with him as he and his wife, Charlotte and their son, Asa, moved from that state through South Carolina into Georgia. From this lineage came descendants of these dogs accompanying Ezekiel and Asa to Lawrence County Mississippi in 1815.

Fifty-eight years later, we find descendants of those animals trotting toward Texas with their masters ever watchful for predators posing a threat to their masters and families. They were absolutely essential to these families who lived far removed from civilization. They served many useful purposes in addition to guarding their owner's property. They made good hunting dogs and would trail anything from a bear to a deer. Cattle and hogs had to be rounded up and penned, and without the dogs, this would have been an impossible task. These animals were much loved by their masters and patiently trotted alongside the wagons all the way to Texas.

My grandfather owned a dog named Bull that accompanied the wagon train to the Big Thicket however after a few weeks he disappeared. They thought a panther or bear had killed him until they got a letter from neighbors back in Jasper County saying Bull had showed up at the old Loftin place near Stringer one evening coated with mud. He crawled upon the porch and lay down with his head pointed toward the front gate. The dog must have gotten homesick, decided the Big Thicket wasn't for him, and backtracked nearly four hundred miles until he reached the old home place. He had to live off rabbits or some other creatures killed along the way and crossed some large rivers. How was this possible? Instinct.

There are other interesting stories about the dogs owned by my Loftin ancestors. More stories await in future pages of this history especially after we reach the Big Thicket where the woods are full of black bear and panther. About the first of May, the wagon arrived at the Benagh Loftin home on Bundicks Creek in Beauregard Parish near DeRidder. Benagh a half-brother to Ezekiel Andrew Loftin had lived in

Sylverena ten miles from Ezekiel for twenty years or more. They had grown close to one another during those years.

However in 1868 he and wife Sarah Stinnett moved with their family to Beauregard Parish in Louisiana near his sister Sinthia and her family. Some of Benagh's sons went into the logging business operating sawmills in that area of the state. One son, William and his son Solomon Loftin, had property along the Sabine River where William's son Murph Loftin operated a ferry called The Loftin Ferry. For a while these Loftins cut pine timber and floated the logs down the Sabine to Orange where they were sold to the large sawmills in and around Orange and Beaumont.

Benagh and family welcomed their relatives from Jasper County and invited them to stay for a few days and rest themselves and their animals. I suspect a fat steer was killed and barbecued and word sent out to l kinsmen in the area to visit with their relatives from Jasper County some of whom they had never met. How long they remained with Benagh? I am not sure but long enough to give their oxen and livestock a chance to regain their strength.

Around the (circa) second week of May the wagon train left Benagh Loftin's home heading for the Big Thicket and crossed the Sabine River on a ferry boat owned by one of Benagh Loftin's sons Murdock Loftin. Within two days they arrived at Old Hardin one of the earliest settlements in Hardin County where they spent the night. A storm came up and lightning killed one of my grandpa's oxen which distressed him so he pleaded with someone to loan him an oxen and he would head back to Mississippi. The next morning the train moved deeper into the Big Thicket finally arriving at the Stacy Collins home located near the Honey Island community

Stacey and Sarah Anderson Collins welcomed their granddaughter Frances, Leonard Lee Loftin and their two children Jane and Amanda. Stacey and Sarah sent word to their sons, Stacey Jr., Warren, Newton and Edward living in the area, who came over to welcome the new arrivals. I suspect they overnight with the men talking and swapping stories until the wee hours of morning Those in the Thicket were thirsty for information about the effects of the war on their countrymen and neighbors back in Jasper and Jones County, and those arriving from Mississippi were interested in land where they could build cabins and settle down to life. There is little doubt the availability of land in the Thicket had been discussed and known by my Loftin ancestors prior to their move to this area of Hardin County.

Since the Collins had some bearing on my grandparents moving to Texas it is appropriate to understand some history of these ancestors. When our children and grandchildren are born we wonder about their mannerisms and looks. The answer is in the genes and chromosomes inherited from preceding generations of our ancestors some more dominant than others. The temperament of my Collins ancestors surfaced clearly among the siblings I grew up with. In the following chapter we take a look at the Collins family however we should keep in mind there is a long line of ancestors on both sides of our families whose genes we inherited contributing to our makeup and our successors. The Collins roots are buried deep in the dense forests of the Big Thicket.

Chapter Five
Collins Kinsmen

Pioneer life has always been much the same; a family pulls up stakes in the hometown and sets out for a new life in a new country. Most of those settling in the Big Thicket were either getting away from something or somebody and what they found was big timber and privacy and the chance to be independent. There weren't many towns near the Thicket when the Collins and Hooks and Harts began coming during the 'forties and 'fifties. There were a few stores in Old Hardin, near present day Kountze, and small settlements at Woodville and Concord a steamboat landing on Pine Island Bayou another at Drews Landing on the Trinity but these places were a long way off for most of the settlers. However the old nesters who came to get some privacy in the Thicket weren't interested in spending much time in town. They liked the lonesome and they wanted to be apart so they could look after themselves.

The Collins came on ox drawn wagons, as did most pioneers during that period. Stacey Jr. and his family had a wagon to carry them and their possessions while Staccy Sr. and Sara Anderson Collins came with their three sons, Newton, Warren and Edwin on another wagon. The men slept outside during good weather and for that reason made the trip during late spring and early summer. Edwin Collins heard there were no poplar trees in Texas so he decided to take some along and plant them. He planted two little poplars in gourds and let them take root before the trip. These were replanted in front of their home near Honey Island and the seedlings grew into large trees. This old home place of the Collins became known as the Old Poplar Tree Place. It took about twenty-five days to make the trip from Jones County, Mississippi to Hardin County.

There was no lumber to build houses, but there were millions of pine saplings the right size for making log houses, the poles notched and laid on each other, then roofed with boards split out of large pines. That was sufficient for building summerhouses but to keep out the cold wind in the winter they cut large pines and rive out sealing boards with a froe. They would cover each one of the cracks between the logs with a sealing board about eight to ten feet in length. When they got the sealing boards nailed they had a very comfortable house. To make it livable they had to have a chimney at one end of the house. Splitting chimney sticks, digging clay out of the ground and mixing it with water then putting the clay all around the chimney sticks made the chimney. They then tapered the chimney from bottom to top in order to draw smoke.

One of the first things to do in a new settlement was put in a farm and raise corn. The only bread these people had at that time was cornbread. The virgin land untouched by human hand was very productive and ten acres of corn would yield all that a family needed during a year. The timber, which covered the land, had to be cleared by hand and it took several years to rid the farm of all timber.

Neighbors from the settlement usually pitched in to assist with the custom of clearing the land and came from miles around to pitch in and help out. Of course when there was a log rolling of this nature the women would gather at the same house and quilt and cook up hearty dinners for the men. They say the best food ever produced was at log rolling which went on from dawn to sunset for three or four days.

Each evening after supper some old country fiddler would tune up his fiddle and rosin up his bow pull the horse's tail across the catguts and the red russet shoes would begin to "come and tip it as they go on the light fantastic toe." They danced as they worked with all their might. By midnight hunger would grip the dancers and a midnight dinner was spread for those who chose to eat. Very little rest would be gotten but at the crack of dawn they would be up and after a breakfast of pork chops and eggs and biscuit's the size of a Stetson hat head for the timber to resume cutting and rolling the logs into piles.

The early settlers' food source came from crops they raised including corn which was ground for their bread and food for their livestock and chickens. Their meat came from hogs roaming the forests supplemented by deer and squirrel thriving in the forests around them. Black bear was numerous about that time and each fall and winter the men hunted and killed the bear for his meat and the lard rendered from the fat of the animal. In the summer they came out of the Thicket to the Piney woods to eat the wild hogs that ranged there.

The Collins men spent lots of time hunting the bear that preyed on their hogs. They butchered hogs in the winter and put them on benches in the smokehouse where the women prepared the meat then salted it away in boxes until it had taken the salt. Then the meat would be cut into strips and hung on sticks in the smokehouse to dry. The women did this because the men were too impatient and usually ruined the meat. Milk came from their cows, which came in fresh each spring and from milk came butter.

The women used spinning wheels and looms to make the cloth material for their clothing. Such was life for the early settlers in the Big Thicket. They provided everything they needed with the sweat of their brow and by gun except coffee beans and salt. Their sugar and syrup came from sugar cane crushed with the juice running into a vat where it was cooked then strained into cans, jugs and buckets. Black can syrup was good eating with biscuits and sausage or pork chops on cold frosty mornings.

Man was not made to live alone and most long to socialize with their fellow man so it was with the early settlers who rode wagons and horses to Old Hardin the county seat about fifteen miles away to meet with other families, swap tales, and play games and sometimes fight. The Collins a competitive people hated to lose most wanting to be leaders of the pack or in games the cock of the walk. Warren Collins was one of those types and stories are still told of his fights with May Hooks or some of his brothers. From what we have been led to believe the fights were hard but cleanly fought and the men remained good friends.

It wasn't these friendly fights that led to the notoriety of Warren Collins and his brothers but their refusal to join the Confederacy in their fight against the Union. All of the sons of Stacey and Sarah Collins came with their parents to Texas except Simuel my great grandfather Collins who died in Jones County, Mississippi.

The family of Simuel and Lydia Collins is shown as follows:

Simuel Collins 1819
Lydia Bynum 1823
Thomas Jefferson 1839
Benjamin Franklin 1841
James Madison 1843
Morgan Columbus 1845
Chaney E. 1847
Harmon Taylor 1849
Frances Abarilla* 1851
*Five more children came later

My grandmother Frances Collins (1851) daughter of Simeon & Lydia Bynum Collins of Jones County Mississippi was only circa ten years old when the war broke out between the North and the South, the so called "Civil War." Frances, one of twelve children, saw her father and several of her brothers join the confederate army and engage in battles against Union forces in their section of the South.

Some of Simeon's brothers also joined the fight against the Union, including Jasper Collins. At some point quite early in the conflict, a large number of Jones County soldiers decided they were poor people fighting a rich man's war. They owned no slaves. All relatively poor. A leader emerged named Newt Knight, who formed a band of circa three hundred ex confederates, including Simeon and several other Collins, and began their own Civil War in Jones County against confederate troops. The story of the rebellion was buried in the southern pages of history following the war until Vicki Bynum and other historians brought it to life during the early years of the twenty-first century.

Simeon who suffered from imprisonment and injuries died in 1865 in Jones County. In 1872, his widow Lydia and several of her sons joined Frances and her husband, Leonard Lee Loftin, in a move to Hardin County Texas. Leonard and Frances settled and raised twelve children while Lydia and several of her sons settled in Polk County. Some graves can be found in cemeteries in these counties. I felt this episode on the early life of my grandmother needed clarification for future readers.

Some of the Collins who settled in Houston County moved to northeast Texas. My grandmother Frances continued to correspond and occasionally visited her Collins kinsmen in northeast Texas. I traced descendants of Markus T.C. Loftin brother of Benagh and grandson of Asa Loftin to the northeast area of Texas and as recently as 1998 had correspondence with one lady a descendant of Markus T.C. Loftin, inviting me to their annual reunion near Crockett. There have been many stories told of the settlers who came to the Big Thicket some true some slightly exaggerated. Among these were the Hooks, Collins, Harts, Bevils, Salters, Jordans, Rosiers, Cushions, Browns, Wiggins, Whitesides, Phelps, Marcontells, Pattersons, Jones, Loftins, and Phelps.

Stories emerging about these families could fill a book however one particular story concerning the Collins is undoubtedly the better known in contemporary circles one has withstood the passage of time. It is the story of Warren, Edwin, Stacey Jr and a few neighbors who gained some degree of notoriety fame by defying conscription into the Confederate Army during the Civil War.

Warren Collins was the leader of this band called by some Jayhawkers. Some of their neighbors who sent sons to fight for the Confederacy I am certain called them something else. The leaders of Confederate detachments sent to capture this band of rebels of course referred to them by other descriptive phrases I choose not to include in this family history.

It began with Texas seceding from the union joining the other southern states against the wishes and recommendation of the man whom all Texans once idolized Old Sam Houston hero of San Jacinto. Houston was adamant in opposing secession saying such a move by Texas and other southern states would be divisive to our union and result in grievous losses of men in this battle. The union should be preserved at all costs and take precedent over any one particular state. We have got to stick together as a nation for if we are divided each faction or state is easy picking by foreign powers. His pleas fell on deaf ears and they not only voted for secession but voted Sam Houston then governor out of office.

When the Collins learned of Sam Houston's refusal to join the secession effort they settled down to live in peaceful tranquility deep in the forests of the Big Thicket. They owned no slaves so why should they fight for others who wanted to continue the practice of slavery. They chose to sit this one out and told the authorities to leave them alone and all would be well.

They again received orders to report to Confederate Headquarters in Liberty to be inducted and assigned to some detachment. They refused so a detachment was sent to arrest them. Several men in the area were arrested and placed in the army.

The Collins men left families for their hideouts along the Polk County line. In this area they had dug wells which supplied their water and food was plentiful, i.e., deer, squirrels along with berries and nuts of all descriptions. Neighbors and kin brought them salt, pepper, coffee, corn and tobacco in water proof bags which was left in trees on a high rise of ground known as Union Wells. In exchange for these supplies the Collins placed the honey in gourds taken from bee trees as payment. This high rise of ground was later given the name Honey Island and became a community.

In time they discovered they could grow tobacco along the bogs and swamps. They cured the tobacco by cutting blocks from trees, placed the leaves in the openings, replaced the blocks using a tourniquet to tighten the block. Within a week or so they had some pretty strong chewing tobacco. I can readily imagine how stout the tobacco must have been. People with great powers of creativity always seem to come up with tobacco, whiskey or other forms of strong libation to stimulate and or satisfy their habits.

For months the Collins remained deep in the forests but finally when word reached them the troopers had returned to Woodville or Liberty they returned to their homes and their families. On one occasion a detachment caught Warren before he could get back into the woods and locked him up in a log cabin in Woodville however during the night using a pocket knife hid in his boot he managed to cut his free and rejoined his sons deep in the Thicket.

A young Confederate Captain Kaiser commander of southern forces at Galveston tiring of the deserters decided to make an end to the Collins. Taking a detachment into the Thicket during the fall of 1863 when the underbrush was dead he encircled the lair of the Collins and set fire to the woods to smoke them out. However the Collins slipped through a break in the ring and went deeper into the woods. This ended the efforts of the confederacy to capture the Collins or so goes the legend. The area burned out there in the Thicket is still called the Kaiser Burnout.

The Collins as mentioned previously were among the first to settle in the Big Thicket during the 1850's and within a short period of time Warren Collins had become the leader of not only his Collins clan but the hooking bull of the county. He was occasionally challenged by other powerful personalities. These differences were normally resolved without knives or guns but with fists or feats of strength.

One family, which threw down the gauntlet to Warren and his brothers, was the Hooks who also settled in the Big Thicket around Old Hardin during the 1850's and became well known for hunting and killing bears. Their reputation spread far and wife even to the halls of the United States Congress and the Supreme Court attracting such personalities to join them in their hunts as Theodore Roosevelt and Chief Justice Hughes.

Legend has it one of the Hooks boys who many claim could outrun the fastest horse in the area named Mae burned the courthouse down at Old Hardin because his family and others wanted the seat of government to be located at Kountze. We don't know if this has any degree of credibility however the new courthouse was not built at Old Hardin but at Kountze and still remains the county seat.

The Warren Collins family was a determined lot having the tenacity and stubbornness comparable to a pit bulldog. Once committed to the fight either physically or orally, they remained in battle to the finish. With words or fists, they were hard to defeat. My friend Ralph Yarbrough imminent congressman from Texas and United States Senator for two terms told me he well-remembered Vinson Collins son of Warren Collins with whom he served in the Texas Senate.

Yarbrough described Vinson as a good man to have in your corner but not as an opponent. Collins never knew the meaning of compromise, which resulted in most of his proposals being defeated. In this Senate body where compromise is a way of life Ralph said V.A. was like a bull in a china closet. He recalled one instance where Vinson wrote a bill enacting a Texas Compensation Law for Workers in the state and made plans to get it on the agenda. This law for the laboring class was long overdue but there were lobbyists for business and employers who bought off key Senators instructing them to kill the bill if they wanted to be reelected.

Vinson devoted days and months on the proposed legislation and succeeded in getting it through the house without too much difficulty however in the Senate it ran into tough sledding. Those Senators supported by powerful lobbyists for big business kept throwing up roadblocks to delay passage keeping the bill in committee where they sought to rewrite the bill to the point where there was little recourse for litigation against negligent employers.

When Vinson saw what was happening he stood in the well of the Senate in Austin, red faced, sweating like his father Warren Collins on the day he fought May Hooks in Old Hardin and launched a tirade against his opponents causing them to squirm in their leather backed chairs. Bellowing with rage he shook his fingers in their faces accusing them of selling out to big business to the detriment of the little man. Sweating from his barrage of accusations they begged for a recess and huddled in their offices.

When the Senate reassembled the chair asked for a vote, which passed, overwhelmingly by acclimation. Yarbrough said he never forgot that moment, and although he and Vinson Collins were often on opposite sides of an issue, they were together that particular day in Texas history the first Workman's Compensation Bill in Texas was authored by Vinson Collins.

I recall family reunions each August on the grounds of the Baptist Church in the Thicket where my father grew up. Dinner was spread on boards nailed between live oaks beside the church and after everyone ate the older people gathered inside the church (no air conditioning) and listened to speakers. Among those who participated was Senator Vinson Collins an old white haired gentleman who described the arrival of the Collins and Loftins in the Big Thicket. He spoke fondly of his cousin Frances Collins Loftin, and their childhood in Jones County Mississippi. I wished I had recordings of those talks by Vinson Collins and other kinsmen who stood in the well of the church and shared an oral history of the Collins and Loftins who settled there in the Big Thicket. Tape recorders had not made the scene at that time.

The annual reunions were discontinued after my father and his brothers and sisters passed away or became too old to promote the reunion. Younger ones became too involved in their own special interests for organizing and perpetuating the events. There was a period during the 1960's and 1970's when no reunions were held, however, in August 1979 after the passing of our brother, James Lee Loftin, my sister Doris and brothers, Harmon and G.C. held a family reunion in Alvin, Texas in 1980 that was so well received we held another reunion there in 1981 for descendants of Leonard Lee Loftin and Frances Collins Loftin. Some two hundred showed up, and after much discussion plans were made to hold the 1982 reunion at Honey Island in Hardin County where our ancestors settled upon arriving from Mississippi in 1873.

I extended a personal invitation to Senator Ralph Yarbrough to be the keynote speaker since he had worked hard on legislation for preservation of the Big Thicket however due to previous commitments was unable to join us. I became acquainted with the Senator through Robert Hawkins an associate of mine and a longtime supporter of Yarbrough. Robert knowing the Senator and I were members of the 97th Infantry Division during WW II although we had never met suggested I drop by his Austin office and pay him a visit.

During a business trip to Austin I went by the senator's office in the Brown Building and found him alone. We talked about our particular units and duties in the 97th. He was with the provost judicial branch while I was a rifleman with Company A 303rd Regiment. I gave him a copy of The Loftin Chronicles and he gave me an autographed book of his life. Before leaving I invited him to kick off our reunion at Honey Island and be our principal speaker however due to previous commitments he could not accept. He wrote a long eloquent letter expressing his congratulations to everyone for keeping their family name and heritage remembered.

I read this letter to the assembled and placed it in the archives of our Loftin history. I also extended an invitation to the 1982 Reunion to Congressman James M. Collins from the Third Congressional District in Dallas, Texas a grandson of Vinson Collins. He declined because of conflicting schedules but was kind enough to write a very informative letter about his Collins kinsmen who settled in the Thicket. In his letter he mentioned his granddad Vinson being a first cousin to my grandmother Frances Collins and his great granddad Warren Collins settling deep in the Thicket. He said their descendants are scattered throughout East Texas including, Woodville, Chester, Livingston. His father Carr Collins was a very devout Baptist and supporter of Baylor University.

I have an article taken from the Dallas Morning News about Carr Collins who made a fortune as the owner of the Crazy Waters Hotel in Mineral Wells, Texas. The water was supposed to cure all stomach disorders along with arthritis and rheumatism and such. People came by the thousands to bath and drink the waters. It was bottled and shipped all over the country along with packages of mineral crystals, which sold like wildfire.

During the depression Carr made millions and later sold the hotel and wells for another million then moved to Dallas where he founded Fidelity Insurance Company and built it into a multi-billion-dollar firm with property holdings over the nation. His sons and grandsons were given a place in the upper crust of Dallas society, which explains their conservative leanings and allegiance to the GOP. Stacey and Sarah Anderson who settled in the Thicket in 1852 had no way of knowing their descendants would become wealthy and famous in the political affairs of their state and country.

I often laugh thinking what would have happened if Ralph Yarbrough a yellow dog Democrat and James Collins a dyed in the wool Republican had accepted my invitation to the 1982 Reunion at Honey Island! It would have been interesting! I wish it could have been but both now are gone to their rest, Yarbrough passed first followed by Collins a few years later.

Congressman Collins thanked me for the Loftin Chronicles although he indicated he was unaware his kinsmen were called Jayhawkers and rebelled against induction into the service on the side of the Confederacy. These Collins were a people of great resolve and courage in carrying out their convictions. You may disagree with them on issues they espoused but you could not help but respect them for their stand on those issues. The Collins kinsmen we are talking about in this chapter came from strong Scottish ancestors who fought for their independence from English rule and through the centuries developed a desire to make their own way in the world without assistance from anyone especially the government. This attitude led them to live by the sweat of their brow and ingenuity. What they could not grow with the plow and hoe nor take with the gun they did without.

Stacey Artist Collins and Sarah Anderson came from this lineage and as a result of their putting down roots in Hardin County in 1852 their descendants are now spread over all of southeast Texas and the country as a whole. Some of their traits were obviously passed down to other generations as evidenced by mannerisms of some of the siblings the author grew up with. Some traits quite admirable however there are others not so desirable. Stacey Artist Collins born in Spartanburg, South Carolina October 18, 1776 died in Hardin County Texas in 1855. He married Sarah Anderson born near Atlanta, Georgia who delivered the family described previously. Sarah also died in Hardin County in the 1855 year and she and her husband are buried in the Collins cemetery near Votaw.

Also in this cemetery near his parents is their son, Edwin W. Collins born in Jones County, Ms. March 20, 1840 and died at Sabine Pass, Jefferson County 1862. Note: CSA records show this Collins died January 5, 1862 at Liberty, Texas. There appears some contradiction here since we were of the opinion Edwin joined his brothers, Stacey Jr., Warren and Newton, in opposing conscription by the Confederacy. The record here of his burial states he served in the Army of the Confederacy. It doesn't say he was killed in the war but there was a battle at Sabine Pass where a number of confederates were killed.

This information is from Cemetery Records of Hardin County compiled by The Southwest

Genealogical and Historical Society of Beaumont, Texas around 1950. This record shows several Collins buried in Felps Cemetery near my parents, sister, brother, grandparents and numerous aunts and uncles. The cemetery is less than a mile from where my Loftin grandparents settled along Pine Island Bayou in the spring of 1873.

The following chapter is about my great grandmother Elizabeth Dyess Loftin and the families who accompanied her to Hardin Co. in 1873. We are able to present a fairly good understanding of Elizabeth and sons, Andrew, Ezekiel, Thomas and Leonard after they arrived in the Big Thicket in Hardin County, however, tracing the lives of the other four sons, John Charles, Giles, Albert and James was much harder. I offer some theories concerning these four sons and where they lived out their lives.

Chapter Six
Elizabeth Loftin and Sons

There is little doubt in my mind the Loftin wagon train stopped at Benagh Loftin's place in Beauregard Parish on their way to Hardin County. Benagh and his half-brother Ezekiel (Zeke). Loftin were close neighbors in Jasper County, Mississippi. Benagh lived in Sylverena only ten or so miles from Zeke's home near Stringer.

After Zeke died Benagh moved to Bundicks Creek near DeRidder, Louisiana to be near Sinthia (Cynthia) his youngest sister and Mark his youngest brother. Benagh had raised these two siblings after their parents died. Sinthia, after her first husband was killed in the Civil War, married Isaac Hall and moved to Beauregard Parish Louisiana. This background information on Benagh and Ezekiel leads me to believe Ezekiel's widow (Elizabeth) and sons stopped for a few days to rest and visit with their kinsmen.

My father told me he had been told by his father that his youngest brother Jimmy (James) returned to Louisiana to court a young girl he met when the wagon train came through that state on the way to Hardin County. In reconstructing a history, threads of information much like pieces of a jig saw puzzle must come together to complete the picture. Much like I have done in figuring out what happened to my Loftin kinsmen who came to Texas from Mississippi.

My father told this story about his uncle Jimmy whom he never met or knew during a visit to our home in Waco during the late 1970's. This Jimmy had to be James his father's youngest brother. This story concerning James (Jimmy) took on added meaning later when I was reviewing old correspondence from Gladys Loftin Baer of Crocket, Texas daughter of Millard Loftin. Gladys was much into genealogy so we had occasion to exchange information quite frequently.

Her letter of July 1989 mentioned several Loftins living in Houston County one named James or J.W. whom she had never met. She had been invited to their annual Loftin reunion however had been unable to attend. The knowledge of these Loftins became more important when tracing the lives of James and Albert the two youngest sons of Elizabeth Loftin

After poring over this data about James and Albert, I came to believe both married and settled in northeast Texas, raised families and lived out their lives. Gladys Loftin who was raised near Pennington knew several Loftin families were living near Apple Springs a small community near Crockett but had never met any of this clan so was uncertain if they were kin. We also had correspondence with genealogists regarding members of the Markus TC Loftin and discovered members of his family moved from Louisiana to northeast Texas around the turn of the century and settled in Trinity County. This bit of critical data was helpful later on in solving the question of why two orphan children of John Charles Loftin returned to Trinity County to live out their lives.

Giles Loftin (1845) fourth oldest son of Ezekiel

and Elizabeth Loftin was the most difficult to trace. I have no evidence he came with the wagon train to Texas. Leonard Harmon Loftin my oldest brother knew a man named Walters a residence of Old Hardin in Hardin County who told him he was a grandson of Giles Thomas Loftin and grew up in Mississippi. One Christmas circa 1901 he along with his father and grandfather Giles Loftin visited Giles' brother Leonard Lee Loftin and his family in Thicket, Texas. Walters said Leonard Loftin and four children were present as his wife and some of the older children were visiting kinsmen in Trinity County. They spent four or five days with Leonard our grandfather before returning to Mississippi. Harmon said Walters often repeated the story without deviating one iota.

This tends to confirm my suspicion Giles either remained in Mississippi or returned there shortly after arriving in Hardin County with his mother and brothers. This leaves only one of the four missing sons John Charles the third oldest unaccounted for however information given to me by a descendant of this Loftin provided evidence as to what happened to him after deserting the army and heading for Indian Territory. We offer the following information regarding these sons of Elizabeth and what happened to each after leaving Mississippi. We know four certain four of these boys settled down in the Thicket.

ANDREW JACKSON LOFTIN the oldest son was wounded in the Civil War and walked with a limp the rest of his life. In the Thicket he was called Cripple Jack Loftin but actually became one of the great bear hunters in the Big Thicket. He was not as well-known as Ben and Bud Hooks who gained reputations far and wide as hunters of the Big Thicket. The Hooks became famous in Hardin County as a result of oil discovered on their land making them more or less wealthy enough to spend most of their time hunting and entertaining celebrities, including President Theodore Roosevelt and Chief Justice Hughes of the Supreme Court, at their hunting lodge in the depths of the Thicket.

The national press accompanied these famous people and while sitting around the campfire in the evening at the Hooks camp they were told tall tales of bear hunts by the Hooks. The legend of the Hooks grows greater with each publication and release by the large city newspapers thirsting for human-interest stories about the Big Thicket. Legends increase with each story related about ancestors and eventually these men are placed on pedestals as heroes. The more often a story is told the greater becomes the legendary accomplishments whether a hunter in the Big Thicket or Davy Crocket in the Alamo. Andrew Loftin was wounded during the Civil War possible Vicksburg within a hundred miles of his home in Jasper County. He was certainly old enough to carry a gun or serve in some capacity during this conflict.

EZEKIEL LOFTIN second oldest son settled ten miles southeast of Honey Island near the community of Saratoga. As far as we can determine this is where Ezekiel (Zeke) lived his life. It is interesting to note one of Zeke Loftin's girls named Martha married Lit Patterson, a fire and brimstone preacher in Hardin County. Martha and Lit Patterson had several children, including Clara who married George Harrison Jones.

From this marriage came several children among whom was a girl named Ethel who died in 1926 and her brother George Jones who went on to fame as a country western singer. Ethel is buried in Felps Cemetery near the graves of my parents and grandparents. Ezekiel Loftin (1840) oldest brother of my grandfather Leonard Lee Loftin (1849) was a great grandfather to George Jones. (My three sons—Don, Tim and Shane—are great grandchildren of Leonard Lee Loftin and George Jones is the great grandson of Ezekiel Loftin.)

THOMAS LOFTIN, fifth oldest son, and his wife Martha came on the wagon train to Texas. I am not sure where they first lived, however, in time, they also settled near Saratoga. My father often spoke of his Uncle Tommy Loftin and wife Martha who died four days after her husband. They are buried in the Holland Cemetery along with their son Oscar and his wife Mamie Loftin. Mamie in her late eighties while attending the Loftin Reunion at Honey Island in 1982 had some interesting stories to relate concerning our ancestors there in the Thicket. She died in an auto accident in 1991 and was laid to rest beside Oscar. I feel fortunate having known Mamie Loftin and thank God for bringing her into our lives to share with us our common heritage.

JOHN CHARLES LOFTIN, the third oldest son, dropped out of sight in 1863 during the siege of Vicksburg and vanished into the pages of history until reappearing forty years later in Hardin County. A descendant of John, Lou Mayo of Farewell, Louisiana, came to my home in Waco during the mid-1990's and exchanged data on our Loftin kinsmen.

Included was information concerning his service in the confederacy. John served in the Confederate Army with Company A, Seventh Battalion Mississippi as a private. He enlisted May 3, 1863 and appears on a list of casualties from Hebert's Brigade at the siege of Vicksburg from May 17 to July 4, 1863. His military record shows he was reported missing on May 17 on a march from Snydar, Mississippi.

Mayo researched the county files of Jasper County and discovered John Charles Loftin married Lucinda Sanders June 12, 1863 and then both disappeared or it is so believed headed for Indian Territory now Oklahoma. He must have decided the war was over as far as the Confederacy was concerned so he went home, took his wife, and left for Indian Territory where they could lay low until the war ended.

We make assumptions here concerning this man and only arrived at these conclusions based on records available. According to Mrs. Mayo Lucinda, Sanders was the daughter of Colonel William and Celia Sanders next-door neighbors to Asa Loftin the grandfather of John Charles Loftin. With the loss of Vicksburg, I am certain there were numerous desertions from the Confederate Army including John Charles Loftin.

Sarah Seawilla Loftin Ainsworth a great granddaughter of John Charles Loftin gave the following information about John Charles Loftin to Lou Mayo

John Charles Loftin and wife Lucinda had six children, three sons and three daughters. Grandmother Lucinda died around 1884 and was buried in Indian Territory. The following year John Charles Loftin headed for Hardin County Texas. Their trip took about two years or more with John having to stop and work for different families to keep his small family in food. Two daughters married lasting nearly two years, and two daughters married brothers living in Livingston, Texas. Another son married and put down roots while another son died, leaving John Charles with two children, Samuel Lazarus Loftin (11) and Gertrude (9) to complete the journey to Honey Island Texas.

Obviously John Charles Loftin came to this area with his children because he wanted to see his mother and oldest brother Andrew who had settled there in 1873. I am not sure if he reached her before she passed away for she would have been in her early eighties. I sincerely hope she lived to see her third oldest son and two of her grandchildren. According to Seawilla Loftin, Ainsworth, her grandfather, built a log cabin near Honey Island where they lived until John Charles Loftin died of pneumonia circa 1888.

These two children Samuel Lazarus (14) and Gertrude (12) packed clothes with food and walked north sleeping by day as if they were afraid of being caught. (We assume they had been living with their uncle Andrew Loftin after their father's death and for reasons unknown to us if Seawilla's story is correct they became displeased with their situation and fled the area leaving under cover of darkness. According to the story these two children continued walking north for about twenty-five miles when they came to a house where the owner fed and gave them shelter for the night.

They remained there working for the family where Gertrude married a man named Pete Gallion. Samuel stayed with the family until he was twenty-one years old then moved north to Sumter, Texas where he met and married Ellen Ainsworth in the Post Oak Methodist Church. Ten children were born to the couple the last,

Samuel Lazarus Loftin, born one week after his father died at the age of 37. He is buried in Chita Cemetery in Trinity County.

(I have a picture of Samuel Lazarus Loftin, his wife, and two small children given me by Gladys Loftin Baer of Crockett, Texas.) This is intriguing information concerning John Charles Loftin after he disappeared from Stringer Mississippi. It seems reasonable to assume he wanted his mother to know these grandchildren. Realizing his death was imminent due to tuberculosis he knew his brother Andrew or one of his brothers living nearby would care for his two young children in case of his death. He had been away from his mother and family since 1863 and wanted to see them once again and die near them. I am not sure if he got there in time to see Elizabeth his mother before she died.

My great grandmother Loftin died prior to my father's birth in 1878 probably around 1876. Apparently John Charles her wayward son arrived in the Thicket after her death but may have spent two or more years with Andrew his oldest brother near Honey Island. Andrew and family assisted him in building a cabin for himself and his children and buried his brother near their mother Elizabeth.

The gravesites of these Loftins disappeared long ago due to neglect, which allowed the Thicket to obliterate their resting places. I hope John Charles Loftin was able to reunite with his mother but seriously doubt this happened however he must have been pleased to reunite with his close kin prior to his passing. Only God has the answers to this.

One aspect of Seawilla's story intrigues me. Why

would the young orphans , Samuel and Gertrude strike out after their father's death under cover of darkness and begin making their way north eventually settling in northeast Texas. They surely had a destination in mind when they set forth under cover of darkness or were they wanting to leave their environment? Quite an interesting story to see how families chose certain paths to follow during the course of their lives.

ELIZABETH DYESS LOFTIN
(1805- 1880)

I am grateful to this lady for bringing her family to Texas for in so doing she opened the door for many of us to make our appearance on earth. This would not have happened if she had chosen to remain in Jasper County or find another place to put down new roots. I believe Elizabeth lived in or near her oldest son, Andrew, and his family near Honey Island and died there during the early 1880's. My father was born in 1887 well after the passing of his grandmother and could offer little information about her.

Her place of burial disappeared over a period of time due to neglect of family who failed to preserve the last resting place of their mother. My father said his dad often told him his grandmother was buried along Indian Creek between Honey Island and Kountze. He told of a trip by wagon to Kountze with his dad as a youngster and remembers camping out on the return trip by a creek between Kountze and Honey Island. While eating their supper over a camp fire, his father said "Son, your grandmother Loftin is buried somewhere along this creek." The following morning they walked up and down the creek for almost a mile in either direction without coming across any discernible grave site or markings. The encroachment of the Big Thicket if not checked with quickly cover what man has built including last resting places of loved ones. Doesn't take too long!

After Dad retired in 1952 he and my brother Leonard Harmon searched for her gravesite several times during the 1960's and early 1970's but never located any signs of a grave or graveyard along the creek. The site like so many others had been lost due to negligence of family members and others who failed to preserve such historic landmarks not to mention cleaning and caring for the graves.

What a tragedy! Such an important link to our past one who played an important role in the move of the Loftins to Texas now lies in a grave in the heart of the Big Thicket known only to her and God. How could her sons living nearby sit idly while their mother's gravesite was obliterated in time by the encroachment of the thicket? Surely they could have placed a marker over the grave and occasionally cleaned the gravesite.

This concerned my father as he believed in preserving the gravesites of family members and spent considerable time caring for the graves of his parents, brothers, sisters and other kinsmen in Felps Cemetery. I recall walking with my dad through Felps Cemetery so many times through the years visiting the graves of loved ones pausing at the site of each grave identifying who was buried there. Some of the names on the weather beaten headstones at the head of their graves were almost indiscernible and some graves marked only with bricks to indicate a gravesite. He would point to three bricks in a row near his parents' graves and say there lays two of my sisters, Lydia, Matilda and brother Zeke their graves marked by red worn bricks.

When my mother died in 1958, my father went to a funeral home in Kountze and purchased a large granite headstone with her name, dates of birth and death etched deeply in the blue granite. In time, he joined Mother there in Felps. Years later visiting the cemetery I was surprised to see granite headstones on the graves of my grandparents and the three siblings named above. Dad had the headstones made by a company in Kountze then was at the cemetery when they were placed on the graves. My dad was one of the most conscientious people I have ever known with a strong allegiance and love for family.

What a nice remembrance it would be if descendants of these Loftins placed a monument or plaque at the entrance to Felps Cemetery in memory of Elizabeth Dyess Loftin and her six sons who settled in this area. The words would describe these pioneers as a people in search of a place where their children and grandchildren might realize their full potential and build better lives for themselves. Although Elizabeth Dyess Loftin isn't buried in Felps Cemetery many of her descendants are there who make up two thirds of those interred there. Loftins take up quite a lot of turf there within Felps. Hopefully such a monument will be erected there someday.

Until then, we leave Elizabeth and her descendants resting in the quiet of the dense forests of the Thicket the silence broken only by the occasional rapping of a red headed woodpecker on some dead tree and the south wind blowing warm through the tops of the pines.

In the following chapter our focus will be on Leonard Lee Loftin my grandfather representing the next generation of my Loftin family in America.

Chapter Seven
*Leonard Lee Loftin**
1849-1923

My grandfather Leonard Lee Loftin was born in Jasper County, Mississippi in 1849 the sixth oldest son of Ezekiel and Elizabeth Dyess Loftin. He and Frances Collins were married in this county June 16, 1868. Frances Collins youngest child and only daughter of Simuel Collins grew up in Jones County adjacent to Jasper County.

I haven't the faintest idea how they met or circumstances leading to their marriage. Family members described this grandmother of mine as very outspoken and opinionated whereas Grandfather was soft spoken and a good listener. Knowing these traits of my grandparents, I believe Grandmother was the pursuer in the courtship, however, this is supposition on my part. I never knew my grandpa Loftin as he died two years prior to my birth, but I was able to visit many times with my grandmother in her home where she lived with Paley and Willis, two of her youngest children. I was also present in the home when she died.

My Loftin grandparents farmed land near my great grandfather Ezekiel and Elizabeth Loftin and older brothers Andrew, Ezekiel, Giles and Thomas in Jasper County. This was immediately following the close of the Civil War and times were rough.

In April 1869, Grandmother gave birth to their first child, Paula Jane, followed by Frances Amanda in November 1871. Their third child Stacey Artist was born in Thicket, Texas in September 1874. These dates proved helpful in determining a window of time in which my ancestors moved from Mississippi to Hardin County Texas. The story of their move and circumstances that caused the move was described in a previous chapter.

Why did they choose the spring of 1873 for the move? Because this was the best time of the year for travel for women and young children especially since they traveled by oxen drawn carts and wagons. My Loftin and Collins kinsmen were not alone as there were others migrating from the south to the west with some settling in western Louisiana and southeast Texas. A study of conditions in the south following the civil war shows there was considerable migration to Texas during this time.

The Big Thicket is a vast timberland covering several counties in southeast sector of Texas stretching from Polk and Tyler Counties on the north down south where the forests give way to grassy prairies and farm lands reaching all the way down to the Gulf of Mexico. Oil discoveries at Beaumont and Sour Lake led to further discoveries along this vast stretch of coastland and the creation of giant corporations along the southern fringe of the Big Thicket. This rapidly expanding oil and gas industry brought thousands into this area however the pioneers who settled in the heart of the Big Thicket only a few miles away were satisfied to remain there in the woods and live a lifestyle inherited from their parents and grandparents.

When rural electricity was made available to their neighbors at Batson, Sour Lake, Kountze, and Silsbee, my kinsmen in the Thicket were using kerosene oil lamps and pulled their drinking water out of hand dug wells. They farmed enough land to raise food for themselves and their livestock.

Some of my kinsmen never left the Thicket. After marrying they settled down and farmed as their parents had done before them. They lived and died and were laid to rest there in Felps Cemetery. A few of their children ventured out of the Thicket and found a whole new world with one or two getting college educations and working themselves into important positions in giant corporations. I know some of these kinsmen who left the Thicket and did well for themselves and their families however some after retiring went back to live there in the peace and solitude of the great forestland.

THE BIG THICKET

There are as many stories about where the Thicket is as there are about what is in it. In the early days the Big Thicket name was applied to an area of climax forest that was bounded on the north by the Camino Real, on the east by the Sabine River, on the south by the Gulf Coastal prairie and on the west by the Brazos. The Spanish missionaries described the area as an impenetrable wilderness.

The early settlers began moving in on it, however, and found that it wasn't as bad as the stories made it out to be. By the 1840's the Thicket was recognized for what and where it was and the offspring of the first settlers through the years have followed the teachings of their ancestors and their own experiences in establishing the Big Thicket boundaries.

According to historians the Thicket today is about fifty miles long and fifty miles wide however at one time you could easily double these figures in describing the geographical dimensions of the Thicket. The reduction occurred as a result of the timber being cut and land cleared for large ranches and farms from its outer perimeters inwardly. The Thicket begins near the corner post where the Polk, Liberty and Hardin County lines meet, and runs in a south-easterly direction following the Pine Island drainage system to below and east of Sour Lake.

The land is hilly up north of the Thicket in Polk and Tyler Counties and the dirt is red. There are more hickory nut trees and red oaks in these hills than the sweet gum, pin oaks and black gum that grow so easily in the Thicket. And there are more seeps and springs on those hillsides then can be found in the flat land to the south. The water that trickles out of the red hills starts half a dozen or more creeks that opens out into the wide fan top of the Thicket. Menard Creek is the main one and the Thicket traditionally begins in the Menard Creek area but other creeks that start or flow up there at the beginning are Mill Creek, Meetinghouse Branch, Beaver Creek, Little Pine Island, Union Wells, Bad Luck, and Big Sandy. And there is legend in every one of them.

The most important body of water in the Big Thicket is Pine Island Bayou. It begins rather weakly in the spring creek area in the northwest part of Hardin County and strains itself through cypress knees all the way down through the Thicket till the woods play out at the Black Creek junction in the rice fields northwest of Beaumont where the bayou spills its water into the Neches River. The Thicket at one time covered six counties today reduced to four counties.

The history of the Big Thicket goes back to the time when it was covered with water. In the last sixty million years, "recent times" according to geologists, the Gulf shoreline of Southeast Texas submerged and emerged time after time, in unison during the Pleistocene Age with periodical glaciations to the north. The shore line that contained the thicket rose above the waters of the Gulf during the Ice Age, and was built up by silt washed down and deposited by some ancestral Trinity River.

The woods of the thicket grew, and ten thousand years ago the thicket dwellers included mastodons, elephants, the American horse, Taylor's bison, camels, tapirs, and giant sloths, beavers and armadillos. Preying on these animals were the saber-toothed tiger and the dire wolf. The time of the glaciers established varieties of soils and vegetation in the thicket that remained after the glaciers retreated, and produced a unique biological crossroads of at least eight different kinds of plant communities.

The Big Thicket is possibly the most biologically diverse area in the world. Cactus and ferns, beech trees and orchids, camellias and azaleas and four carnivorous plants all occupy what is called the thicket, along with pines, oaks, and gums common to the rest of East Texas.

The thicket supports a wide variety of animal life and is especially noted for the many species of birds, around three hundred and fifty that either live in the area or visit annually. The abundant rainfall and the long growing season, around two hundred and forty-six days, ensure that vegetation and all animal life that depends on it thrive.

Three groups of Indians are associated with the early history of the thicket. They are the Atakapas, the Caddos, and the Alabama-Coushattas. In the historical beginning only the Caddo and the Atakapas moved through the thicket with any regularity. Other tribes from as far away as Oklahoma, Colorado, and Kansas made periodic hunting trips into the thicket for bear meat, skins and tallow. The Tonkawas, Lipans, and Wichitas met in peace at the medicinal spring around what is now called Sour Lake. But primarily the thicket was the meat house of the mound building Caddos, who occupied the fertile rolling hills to the north, and the cannibalistic Atakapas, who bounded the thicket on the Gulf Coast and on the Trinity River bottoms. At the end of the eighteenth century, the Alabamas and Coushattas began to settle on the northern and western fringes, and the thicket and the woods became theirs.

The first man to lay a personal claim to the area was Lorenzo de Zavalla whose 1829 Mexican land grant included the Big Thicket. No Mexicans came, however, and the first settlers to move into the thicket area were Anglo-Americans who began moving into Southeast Texas in the 1830's. The first settlers stopped on the edge of the Thicket, but soon the Thicket itself was spotted here and there with log cabins with people who lived off the land as naturally as their Indian neighbors. These are the people that are still there, in blood and genes if not in the flesh.

The core of the Thicket population is still white,

Anglo-Saxon, and Protestant. The black population within its boundaries is small. The thicket did not lend itself to plantation farming and the slaves and field hands that went with it. There are a few Cajuns on the southwestern edge, in the Batson Prairie area. There are a few Slavonians left over from the days of tie cutting and stave making, and some "foreigners" stayed behind after they drifted in to work for the big sawmills or during the oil boom. But the natives, the ones whose roots are generations deep in the thicket soil, are Southerners by sympathy and migration; they are conservative politically and socially, and they are protestant fundamentalist in religion.

The economic history of the thicket is much the same as that of the rest of East Texas. Until the 1880's the inhabitants dwelt scattered through the woods and lived off what they raised on subsistence farms. They ran hogs and cattle on a relatively free range and hunted small games, deer, and bear. The lumber industry brought a new economy in the 1880's, cut the virgin pine, and opened up more land to farm and graze.

The Sour Lake oilfield in 1901, then the Saratoga, Batson and other oilfields brought about a period of frantic activity. After the oil booms, life settled back to its normal, rural pace and remained so through the 1930's. World War II and the shipyards of the Gulf Coast brought about the major change in the thicket way of life. Many of those who went to war or the shipyards never returned to the thicket county.

After the war the increasing number of paved roads and cars and power lines funneled in massive doses of the outside world. Except for the most confirmed woodsmen, the bulk of the population is now located in

Kountze, Honey Island, Sour Lake, Saratoga and Batson. So there in the thick forestland of the Thicket is where these ancestors of mine built cabins and where some lived out their lives.

Anyone tracing this Loftin lineage eventually finds themselves in the northwestern sector of Hardin County ten miles south of the Polk County boundary and five miles east of the Trinity County line around settlements of Thicket and Honey Island. Here is where my Loftin grandparents settled to live after arriving from Mississippi in 1873.

They settled on a section of land and cleared a sizeable section of timber and brush where they built log cabins, barns and corrals and planted crops. I have no idea how they came into ownership of this land possibly through homesteading, but they lived there nearly thirty years. This was some of the most beautiful timbered land in the Big Thicket tract which at one time covered over a hundred thousand square miles covering nearly five counties in the southeastern part of Texas.

My grandfather Leonard Lee Loftin and three of his brothers, Ezekiel, Andrew and Thomas lived within a fifteen miles radius of each other. At that time there were four established communities in Hardin County, Sour Lake, the oldest, Honey Island, Old Hardin, Kountze, Saratoga, Batson and Thicket the most sparsely populated settlement where my grandparents settled.

There in the heart of this wild and beautiful wilderness they raised or tried to raise twelve children. Ezekiel age seven died early from pneumonia as did Cynthia at the age of eighteen while their sister, Matilda, died in her teens attempting to birth a child.

All but one of the twelve children would eventually rest with their parents in Felps Cemetery within half a mile of where they grew up. The children's names and dates of birth are shown below.

Paula Jane Loftin	April 19, 1869 Mississippi
Frances Amanda Loftin	November 4, 1871 Mississippi
Stacey Artist Loftin	September 6, 1874 Texas
Elydia Loftin	November 10, 1876 Texas
Ezekiel Loftin	January 10, 1878 Texas
James Millard Loftin	August 26, 1881 Texas
Matilda Loftin	January 13, 1884 Texas
Leonard Harrison Loftin*	May 11, 1887 Texas
George Willis Loftin	October 10, 1889 Texas
Willard Wiley Loftin	October 4, 1891 Texas
Saber Paley Loftin	March 11, 1894 Texas
Benjamin Hector Loftin	March 16, 1898 Texas

Leonard and Frances Loftin assisted by Collins' kinsmen and neighbors cleared land to build a cabin and plant crops essential for themselves and livestock. My kinsmen brought with them the same customs and mannerisms inherited from ancestors in North Carolina during the late 1600's and early 1700's. They planted basically the same crops i.e.; corn, peas, sweet potatoes, and such crops typical of most southern families. Their meat and lard came from hogs butchered each winter and from squirrel and deer roaming the forests about them. They were not the most industrious of people caring little for accumulation of wealth or worrying about tomorrow.

Introverted to a degree they had little concern for what was going on outside in the more or less civilized world in towns such as Beaumont, Sour Lake and

Liberty within twenty miles of where they lived. The only time they ventured outside the Thicket was when a family member became so ill they sent for Doctor Roark in Saratoga seven miles south.

For entertainment and socialization, they rode over to Old Hardin once a month on a Saturday to buy coffee, sugar, salt and stock up on snuff or chewing tobacco and socialize with other families in the area. The boys found ways to entertain themselves as did the men who engaged in contests of strength and skill or racing their horses. Occasionally these contests ended in fistfights while the women spent time gossiping and finding out what was happening in other families.

All of my aunts and uncles dipped snuff, and this habit unfortunately was acquired by my parents as well as my Zorn grandparents. A filthy habit to say the least, however, history shows kings and queens and other royalty sniffed and/or dipped the tobacco. Mom never quit dipping the stuff, however, Dad quit after Mom died but nearly went crazy before he eventually kicked the habit. He was able to do this because of a strong will.

This habit of snuff dipping or chewing came out of the tobacco fields of the south where tobacco was the main agricultural crop grown, and the drying barns were filled with large leaves being cured for shipment back across the pond to the tobacco shops in London. It was quite easy for those working in such an environment to acquire the habit of chewing or smoking the stuff. The study of tobacco is quite revealing.

Early kings and queens carried gold boxes filled with fine snuff, which they sniffed up their nose presumably to clear their nasal passages or sinuses.

This was a dignified custom among royalty whose elevated status forbade the uncouth practice of spitting so they sniffed. The commoners couldn't care less about sniffing so they placed a bit of snuff between their lower lip and gum and let saliva do the rest.

Regardless of how tobacco is used it continues to be one of the filthiest habits a person can pursue and my parents and grandparents on both sides of the fence were addicted to the stuff. The habit is carried on extensively among the modern generation even though it is proven to cause cancer of the lips, mouth and throat.

Women kept a small can of Garret or Tube Rose in the pocket of an apron while the men kept their can in their shirt pocket. The men put a pinch between their gums and teeth while the women used a small sweet gum twig, which they wetted and dipped into the can to pick up sufficient snuff to place in their mouth. Oh how they delighted in sitting on the front porch talking and laughing and feeling the saliva moisten the tobacco in their gums. Occasionally, to relieve the buildup of salvia in their mouths they would spray a stream of the brown liquid in the yard to be absorbed in the sandy loam. Dogs and chickens passing within range of the expectorants had learned from experience to be alert and dodge the oncoming barrages from the porch.

This habit was passed down from generation to generation and they saw nothing wrong with it. No television adds pointing out the inherent dangers of nicotine shortening their lives or warning labels on each product for this would come later to the next generation. The women dipped snuff while openly condemning the evils of drinking moonshine whiskey or Muscatine wine calling those the devil's brew.

The preachers I remember as snuff dippers stood before their congregations and preached the evils of whiskey and rum, then sat down and gorged on fried chicken and all the trimmings until they could hardly walk. There were those who preached fire and hell sermons then slip off behind a grove of oaks and take a snort before coming back to spread good will assuring all concerned they were saved and ready to enter the pearly gates.

The Thicket settlers dug water wells off their back porch convenient to their kitchen. The water was lifted from the well by bucket tied to a rope run through a pulley suspended from the frame over the well. They also placed their milk and butter in syrup buckets and lowered them into the well where they could stay cool and most delectable.

The homes of these settlers were made of cut timber notched and laid on top of each other for the sides and the back. Flat boards called sealing boards cut from logs were placed between the cracks for insulation against the cold of winter. I remember the first time I ever visited the old home site where my father and eight more siblings were born less than a mile from Felps Cemetery.

After attending a funeral service in Felps in 1947, Dad drove us over a winding road which led over Little Pine Bayou and after about a quarter of a mile came parked in front of nice home surrounded by tall pines. Dad said, "Son, this is the place your Loftin grandparents settled on when they came from Mississippi and where I grew up as a boy."

A man, who Dad knew by the name of Williams,

came out, and after talking for a few minutes, Dad said, "I wanted my son to see the cabin where I was born if it still exists."

Williams smiled and led us through a cow lot to two buildings—one new, the other an old log cabin crumbling with age.

Dad stopped in front of the old cabin and said, "Don, this is the cabin where I was born May 11, 1887."

The main room of the cabin although in shambles was still identifiable with a small overhead loft where he said the boys slept. There were two side rooms below where their sisters and parents slept as well as the kitchen where they not only cooked but ate their food.

Walking over a few feet he kicked the soil with his Sunday go to meeting shoes as he called them saying our water well sat about here off the back porch. This was a well hand dug by Paw and some of his older brothers. Paley, Willis, Hector and Wiley (siblings) still use wells off their back porches today

Dad said they had to tote water in large cans and fill troughs for their livestock during drought times from nearby Pine Island Bayou fifty yards from their cabin. His paw also built a pen in the edge of the Bayou where the horses and mules and milk cows and calves drank without getting loose to run in the woods.

I never forgot that trip to the birthplace of my father that day in 1947. Forty years passed before I would return to that site.

Don H. Loftin

A WALK DOWN MEMORY LANE

In October 1987, Shane, my youngest son, and I, with his friend Clinton Anderson, visited Leonard Harmon, my oldest brother, at his home near Sour Lake. Shane and Clinton spent their time hunting. Harmon and I caught up on talking and reminiscing.

Harmon's home was located in the southern fringe of the Big Thicket two miles northwest of Sour Lake. One day, we drove up to Thicket and visited the gravesites of our parents and kinsmen in Felps Cemetery. Afterwards, we drove by the site where our parents lived after moving from Pennington in 1920. Of course, the home was no longer there. Then we drove past Felps Cemetery and over Pine Island Bayou to the birth place of our father.

The property was then in the possession of R.J. Williams, whose father I met in 1947. He welcomed us as had his father forty years before. I told him of the history I was working on and wanted to learn more about my father's birth place, especially the cabin he was born in.

Williams smiled, then led us around a corral where several horses were standing. In the far corner was a large tin barn. We entered the barn and walked to the opposite side before what obviously were the remains of an old log cabin.

Harmon and I looked at each other, overcome with emotion, struggling to maintain our composure. Williams said he was well aware of the history of this cabin and not wanting to destroy it had the new barn built over it.

Placing a hand on one of the logs, Williams said,

"This heart of white pine is as solid as the day it was notched and set in place over a hundred years ago, actually one hundred and fourteen years ago."

This was a moment in time I will always remember and cherish. I never returned to this old site but through time wondered if it still exists.

R.J. Williams sent me an Abstract Title (copy) of this property on file in Hardin County Courthouse in Kountze, which reads: 2/27/908 Charles Dillingham 200 acres to William Lumber Company/ 9/14/15 William Lumber Company 40 acres to S.L. Whitson. 5/14/37 Whitson willed to Wylie Loftin 40 acres. Mr. Whitson elderly resident of the Thicket was cared for by Wylie and Myra Rosier Loftin during the last years of his life and bequeathed them this forty acre tract of land. On 5/17/46 Wylie Loftin sold 40 acre tract to A. E. Williams who deeded the property on 10/5/54 to his son R.J. Williams. Mr. Williams mailed the letter from Saratoga February 25, 1988 the year following our visit to his place October 1987.

Harmon said his uncle Wiley Loftin offered to sell him the forty acres after he came home from the service in World War II for five dollars an acre, but he turned it down thinking he could not afford to look after the property. Foolish man! The property is worth thousands of dollars today in the heart of the largest body of hardwoods and pines on the North American Continent. What a treasure it would have been for descendants of L.L. Loftin. The pine timber alone was worth thousands.

My father and the other siblings worked along their father and the older men, There was a four room schoolhouse built in 1895 about two miles from the

Loftin place the children attended during the winter months. They could not attend during the spring and summer since fields were prepared for planting in the spring and crops harvested during late summer and early fall. In late autumn, the children began school, which continued through the winter. My father told of his older brothers and sisters walking to school each morning and crossing nearby Pine Island Bayou on a log serving as a footbridge.

One morning on their way to school, they came to the log bridging the creek, and one of the boys saw a panther crouched on a low limb hanging over the creek. He quickly called out to the others to turn back. Running to the house, they alerted their parents and his uncle Andrew (Cripple) Jackson Loftin who was visiting with his brother.

The men, with their guns and dogs, went to the crossing and the dogs trailed and treed the cat. Jackson shot the panther that measured about six feet in length. There were panthers and bears in the Thicket during that period of time, however, by the early 1900's most of them had been killed out. I believe the last black bear killed in Hardin County was around 1915. Incidents such as the one described made the children more aware of their surroundings in the future and cautiously studied the environment at all times.

Leonard and Frances Loftin lost three children early—Lydia, Ezekiel, and Matilda. Elydia Loftin (1876) a lovely girl fell in love with a young man named Smith and became pregnant with his child. Both she and the baby died during childbirth. Those who remember say she was really a pretty girl, quite headstrong. A red brick was the only marker for her grave. After my father retired from Gulf, he bought granite markers and had them placed on the graves of Ezekiel, Lydia, Matilda, and his parents. Ezekiel (1878) died when he was about seven years of age from pneumonia.

Dad never knew Little Zeke, however, he was told his father and an uncle made his coffin out of white pine lined by the women with velvet material. He said his father carried Zeke's coffin by horseback the half mile to Felps Cemetery where they placed him beside Elydia, his sister.

Matilda Loftin (1884) died giving birth to a child fathered by a Sid Smith, I understand. Both she and the baby died during this birth. She was also buried by Lydia and Ezekiel. Her parents would be buried at the head of the graves of their three young children. Matilda must have been a special sister to my father since he spoke with affection as we walked among the graves in Felps Cemetery. In a family of twelve, those nearest in age tend to form closer ties while growing up.

The remainder of the twelve children in this family lived long lives, several into their eighties and two into their nineties. They were free from most pressures as we experience them today. Their main concern was living from one day to the next. Television had not made its appearance at that time, bringing the troublesome news of the world into our living rooms, nor the rapid age of communications creating a society on the run. No my aunts and uncles remained in the Thicket, working their patches (gardens), raising enough to live on. Some raised grandchildren while their sons and/or daughters left to work in the oilfields around Batson or Sour Lake. The old timers still clung to the customs and habits formed by a lifetime of carving a living out of the environment around them.

Some of my aunts and uncles were still drawing water out of the hand dug wells at the edge of their back porches, wells dug fifty years before. As long as they could sit on a stool, they milked a cow or two, which normally came in fresh each spring. The milk for drinking and butter from churning was dangled by rope into the well for cooling.

Chickens running loose around the yard and/or in the woods around the house provided Sunday dinners when company was anticipated. Sissie, my wife, and my oldest son Don had occasion to visit my kinsmen still living in Thicket, and most were still drinking water lifted by pulley from the well off their back porch.

At our Loftin Family Reunion in July 1982 near Honey Island, the oldest living relative was my Aunt Beatrice Loftin, widow of Benjamin Hector Loftin, youngest child of Leonard and Frances Collins Loftin. She had quite a story to tell to those of us gathered that day and will be described in some detail later in this history.

TO HOUSTON COUNTY

In 1903 Leonard Lee Loftin sold out and moved with wife and four of their youngest children to Houston County where he farmed cotton. They raised their food products along with hogs and cattle for their meat and milk and butter. The reason for the move was due to Grandma wanting to live near her Collins kinsman in Trinity County. She was a lady who was hard to say no and usually had her way with Grandpa, we were told. The Collins were stubborn people.

I was told by my father and older brothers that James Millard Loftin (1881), a favorite of his mother, persuaded both of his parents to make the move from the Thicket. Millard inherited the traits of his mother and her Collins side of the family. He was an independent sort and roamed the Thicket looking for excitement and companionship.

When only a mere boy of seventeen, he rode alone north eighty-five miles to spend time with some of his Collins kin in Trinity County. From what I have been told, Millard was a strong favorite of his mother who wanted to join her Collins kinsmen in Trinity County, but Grandpa Loftin refused to move, saying he was more than content there in the Thicket. He had not only a good farm but forty acres of timber, some of which was virgin longleaf pine. Grandma kept after her husband to move, but he held out until soon after the turn of the century. I have included a letter from a first cousin of mine describing the influence of her father Millard Loftin in convincing his parents to move up to Houston County.

The following information on the Leonard Lee Loftin family was given to me by Gladys Loftin Baer, during our family reunion in Crockett, Texas July 13, 1987. Gladys was the second oldest child of James Millard and Viola Collins Loftin born in Houston County who spent most of her later life in Crockett. She died in 2002 near her ninetieth birthday.

Gladys said her father, at the age of eighteen, would ride by horseback ninety miles to visit Collins kinsman in Houston County. In 1902, he worked on a farm owned by a man named Sheffield and, during this time, found out Sheffield was putting the farm up for sale. Millard informed his parents the farm was up for sale and urged them to buy the place. They sold their property in the heart of the Big Thicket in 1903 and moved to Houston County to the Sheffield place with their four youngest children, Leonard, Willis, Paley, and Hector.

The oldest children Frances Amanda and Paula Jane then married to brothers, Amanda to John Swearingen and Paula Jane to Lit Swearingen, and remained in the Thicket for a year or so before selling out and moving to Houston County. Stacey Artist and Wylie had also married and raised families in the Thicket. Wylie Loftin never left, however, Stacey, in later years following the death of his wife, was struck and killed by a log truck while visiting one of his children, around Kirbyville I believe. Stacey was blind in one eye as a result of a cow hooking him in that eye while in the process of milking her one morning. Stacey, Wylie, their wives, and most of their children rest in Felps.

According to Gladys Baer, Leonard Harrison, Willis, Paley, and Hector attended the same school in Pennington, which is reasonable as there was only one school where children of all ages were taught reading, writing, and arithmetic.

Willis Loftin, the youngest, enlisted in the Calvary during World War I but never went overseas. We have pictures of him in his uniform by his mount. During his lifetime, he never strayed far from the side of his mother and, with her passing, spent the remainder of his days with Paley, his widowed sister and her three children.

The two oldest children Jane and Amanda, the only children born in Mississippi, married Swearingen brothers and followed their parents to Houston County where they farmed for a few years. About 1908, they relocated to Cleveland in Liberty County for a year or so before moving back to the Thicket settlement where they went into the logging business. Paley, youngest sister of Jane, and Amanda also lived in Cleveland with her parents until the death of her father in 1923 whereupon she moved with her mother to Thicket.

Leonard and Jimmy Loftin, with their three children, moved from Trinity County in 1920 to the Thicket settlement in Hardin County. Dad sold his farm in Pennington to Jap Brannon and Jim Dominy who gave the place to one of their girls when she married. My parents lived in Thicket five or six months before moving to the Batson community where Dad found work with Gulf Oil Company. My brother James Lee and I were born in Batson.

Leonard and Frances Collins Loftin and their son Willis eventually moved from Pennington to Cleveland where their daughter Paley was living with the Swearingen families. She eventually moved in with her parents, and from that time on, she was the prime caretaker for her parents until they passed.

Benjamin Hector Loftin, the youngest of the twelve children of Leonard Lee Loftin, married Beatrice Golden, a Trinity County girl, and remained in northeast Texas for several years but eventually returned to Thicket where he and Aunt Bea raised three children, Marie, Bernice and Leonard.

Millard, six oldest Loftin of the children, stayed in Houston County and raised a family of seven children including, Gladys Loftin Baer who provided me with a great amount of the history and background of our Loftin families. After their children were grown, Viola Loftin, tired of Millard and his gallivanting, told him to leave. He began visiting brothers and sisters around the country and, while visiting with Wiley and Paley, was killed by a speeding car one evening as he walked between their homes. The driver said he never saw him. I believe Millard was buried around Alto beside his first wife. He was the only one of the twelve children of Leonard Lee and Frances Loftin not buried in Felps Cemetery.

My Loftin grandparents moved to Cleveland, Texas during the First World War where their two oldest daughters, Jane and Amanda Swearingen were living with their husbands who were engaged in the lumber industry. They had rented a home near town where they were living with their daughter, Paley, and son, Willis, when he died of a stroke near the end of October in 1923.

My brother, George Calvin (G.C.) Loftin, in a letter of August 8, 1987, described the passing of our Grandpa Loftin. G.C., eight years old at the time, with his brother Harmon and father visited their grandparents in Cleveland, Texas in October 1923. "Dad, Harmon, and I, in our Model T Ford, drove from Batson to Uncle Wiley Loftin's home in Thicket where we spent an hour or so before driving on to Votaw where, after parking their car, they waited for the train to come by. No station was available so the train had to be flagged down. After waiting an hour or so, the train came chugging down the tracks, and Dad stepped out on the track and, with his handkerchief, flagged the train down. They boarded and Dad paid the conductor as the train moved on toward Cleveland, arriving there around midafternoon.

They walked to the house where our grandparents lived with Paley, their youngest daughter, and Willis, their son. It was a small white house with screened in porches in the front and along one side. Paley came home from work at a downtown café around five, and she and grandma prepared a real fine supper of greens, potatoes, peas, corn, and cornbread with pie to top it off.

They had finished eating and were sitting around the table laughing and talking when Grandpa pushed back from the table saying, "I am going out on the back porch for a smoke" and left the kitchen. Less than five minutes later, they heard him fall. Uncle Will exclaimed, "Paw has fallen!" They rushed out to the porch to find him sprawled out on the floor with his pipe still clenched between his teeth.

Note: This pipe and one other along with two large bull Durham sacks of pipe tobacco were the only items or possessions our family kept that belonged to our grandfather. For years, these items remained in the top of the front bedroom closet in our home in Sour Lake. I recall taking the pipe and studying it from time to time. You could still see the teeth marks on the stem where grandpa bit down as the stroke hit him. In time, the tobacco sacks all rotted away and eventually the pipes disappeared.

Continuing story by G.C.: They picked Grandpa up and carried him into his bedroom and placed him on the bed. Willis ran a few blocks for a doctor who, after examining grandpa, said he had a massive stroke with no hope for survival. Dad told them to go in and see your grandfather for the last time. He died later that evening.

They designated Dad to make funeral arrangements so he went to the train depot and called Monroe Brackin, who had the only phone in the Thicket, and asked him to spread the news. Pace Funeral Home would handle the body and carry it to Wiley Loftin's place the following day for viewing.

After spending the night with their grandmother and Paley and Willis, they rode the train to Votaw got in their car and returned to Batson. G.C. was eight and Harmon was ten at the time so Grandpa died in 1923 at the age of seventy-five. This ended G.C's explanation of the death of our Grandpa Loftin in his letter of August 31, 1987.

Friends and kinsmen who had known Leonard Lee Loftin came from all over the Thicket and Hardin County to pay their last respects. Two days later, they carried his body to Felps where he was buried near his three children, Lydia, Ezekiel, and Matilda. He had lived on this earth for seventy-five years and was now free from the burdens of life with all of its worries and heartaches. The sire of twelve children, most of whom would live long lives.

Following Grandpa's passing, Grandma Loftin moved with Paley and Willis from Cleveland to Thicket where they lived in a home owned by her son Wiley. The house where my grandmother died and where Aunt Paley and Uncle Will continue to live in until their deaths was first a log cabin, however, over time siding was added. There were two white oak trees in front of the home where Grandma, Aunt Paley, and Uncle Will lived, and us kids would strain our eyes and watch for the sight of the tree limbs hanging out near the roadway when we drove up to visit.

The road passing in front of my grandmother's house was deep sand, an impediment to traffic and hard to maneuver though so it was not unusual to see a car mired down in the middle of the road sunk up to the wheel hubs in sand. However, in time and the coming of new technology during the 1960's, this road through the Thicket became a paved highway actually a racetrack for cars and trucks.

Another road intersecting the main road in front of their home leads to the Felps Cemetery about a half mile north where my grandparents, parents and eleven other siblings are buried. The road leading to the cemetery is seven miles north of Saratoga.

THE PASSING OF MY GRANDMOTHER
FRANCES LOFTIN

I will never forget the passing of my grandmother Loftin who really suffered during the last year of her life with tuberculosis of the bone (cancer). All of her family gathered where she was then living with Paley, three of Paley's children, Ira, Jackie, Frances, and of course, Uncle Will, her bachelor son. All of my dad's family was present. My two older brothers, Harmon and G.C., went up earlier to assist with arrangements.

We arrived about six in the evening. Grandmother was in great pain, and Doctor Roark left morphine to deaden her pain while telling the family she only had a few hours to live. As was the custom, the men squatted on their haunches under the white oaks in front of the house talking, whittling, and dipping snuff.

Around nine p.m., one of the ladies came to the fence saying, "If you want to tell Maw goodbye, better do it now." My father, along with his brothers, passed through the old wooden gate up the oak steps to the porch and entered the bedroom on the right of the living room where their mother lay. The small room filled with people standing around the bed. Me and some of the older children glanced into the room and watched. I must have been around nine at the time.

Then something happened I have never forgotten. Willis, her youngest son in his forties, got up on the bed and took her in his arms, crying for her not to leave him! This set women and children to weeping. My grandmother passed from this life around eleven that evening, as I recall, and the crying and wailing really commenced.

This was typical of what happened when a death occurred among dwellers in the Big Thicket. This habit did not pass down to our immediate family, who mourned the passing of loved ones but better controlled our emotions than our kinsmen in the Thicket.

I can never forget that evening with all the events that unfolded, one being at the death of my grandmother, the howling of the family dogs under the log house. They came from under the porch and began howling the most mournful sound you could ever imagine. What an eerie setting this was! The howling of the dogs continued for about an hour or so it seems.

Soon after she died, some of the women washed the body, placed it on a cooling board, and as was customary positioned it to prevent the body from drawing up into a fetal position making it hard to fit inside the coffin. The ladies then dressed Grandmother in one of her best dresses and Pace Funeral Home of nearby Kountze came for the body.

I, along with several other young cousins, spent the night with Uncle George and Etta Felps who lived only a hundred yards from the Cemetery bearing their name. There were several of us kids ranging in age from five to twelve, and we slept on quilts in the large living room before an open fireplace. Uncle George sat in a wheel chair, a large friendly man, smoking his black pipe while twiddling his thumbs. Back and forth, back and forth, twirling his thumbs and smoking that pipe. I am not sure why I remember so vividly this action by a person I hardly knew.

The following morning Aunt Etta and her daughter prepared a huge helping of eggs, pork chops, gravy, biscuits, ribbon can syrup, and milk. What a sight to watch a table full of kids demolish such delicious food. My parents came by to get me on the way to the cemetery only a short distance up the road. Uncle George Felps died the following year and was buried there in Felps soon followed by wife Etta.

My grandmother was buried that afternoon beside my grandfather Leonard Lee Loftin who died in September 1923. She came to the Thicket in the spring of 1873 and raised twelve children, and after leaving for twenty-five years, she came home to live out her life. She died in March 1935 sixty-two years after she and her family arrived from Mississippi.

She was a remarkable person with a tremendous amount of courage and determination and loved by her children and fiercely protective of her own. Called Puss by her brothers and uncles, she was the boss of her family, loved and admired by her sons, but resented by their wives who were insecure in the presence of their mother-in-law.

I have been told this was the reason my mother insisted my father find work outside of the Thicket. My mother was a kind and patient woman but had a great deal of pride in her ability to care for the needs of her family without anyone telling her what to do. Other daughters-in-law gave in to their mother-in-law, not my mother! So Dad went outside the Thicket settlement, found work with Gulf Oil, and established a little breathing room or space between my mother and her mother-in-law.

There are several interesting stories concerning Grandma Loftin, one told by Beatrice Golden Loftin, wife of Hector Loftin, during the Loftin Family Reunion in Honey Island July 13, 1983. Aunt Bea was in her late eighties as she told the story to a gathering of over a hundred and fifty. This all happened when she and several others spent the night with their mother-in-law while their husbands and Grandpa Loftin left on a trip to buy some horses near Batson.

Prior to leaving for Batson, the men butchered a hog and pulled it up to the limb of a tree in their backyard for it to chill overnight. This was in November and the nights had gotten much colder. The women were going to butcher the hog the next morning, converting some parts into sausages, hams, and sides to be hung in the smokehouse for curing.

By mid-morning the men on horseback were on their way toward Batson prairie about ten miles through the woods. The women spent the day doing routine chores.

Around nine o'clock that evening the children were in bed and the women were preparing to retire when grandma asked everyone to be quiet and listen. In a moment or so, they heard the cry of the panther sounding a long way off. A few minutes later, they heard the scream again much closer, causing the dogs chained under the back porch to begin whining and moving about nervously. The dogs had been chained to prevent them from following the men to Batson.

The creature screamed again much closer and Grandma said it's coming for the hog. By then the dogs were whimpering and hitting against the chains. Grandma went out on the back porch near the dogs, talking to them in a soothing tone, hoping to calm them down.

She and the other women and girls were looking out on the scene from the door leading out on the back porch. As a result of the moon, they could see the hog hanging from the limb of the tree about seventy feet from their back porch. Grandma stepped off the porch and unchained the dogs and the race was on. These were varmint dogs, but Grandpa used them to not only hunt deer and bear but guard their property. The time had come, and they were ready for the challenge.

Down through the cornfield ran the panther with the dogs in hot pursuit, heading north toward the dense brush around Pine Island Bayou. Bea said they could hear the sound as they tore through the dry corn stalks followed by a brief period of silence then an awful commotion when the dogs brought the animal to bay.

Grandma ran by the woodblock where they cut

firewood and yanked the axe stuck in the block free and began running toward the sounds of the battle. The others didn't follow but was told this was what happened according to Grandma afterwards.

When she came on the scene, the panther was backed against the roots of a large sweet gum that had blown over the past spring in a violent lighting storm and was fighting off the dogs. She kept swiping at each dog as it attacked, knocking them backwards. Grandma knew she had to do something or one of the dogs was surely going to be killed or seriously wounded. One dog had already been cut deep along its sides.

As Grandma stood there, another dog took a hard lick, knocking it head over heels, so fearing for the safety of the dogs, she slipped behind the large clay root behind the panther, and while its attention was on the pack, she smote the animal in the head momentarily stunning it. The dogs quickly finished the creature, a mother panther obviously with kittens waiting in their lair for their mother to return to nourish them. This mother had given her life in search of food to sustain her children. Such are the cruel demands Mother Nature often makes of its creatures.

Grandma checked the dogs that were pretty badly mauled, then walked with them back to the house and rubbed their wounds with axle grease. Back at the house, the other women asked Grandma why she hadn't used a shotgun or rifle instead of an axe, and her reply was "I was afraid I might hit one of Paw's dogs, and he'd never have forgiven me if one was killed." For sure dogs had a special place in the lives of families in the Big Thicket during those times.

My two brothers, Harmon and James Lee, had

dogs, either for hunting or chasing fox. Harmon kept a pack of fox hounds mostly blue tick and black and tan while J.L. used his hounds for hunting the buck deer in the deep woods between Jackson Creek and the Black Cat Deer camp located a mile north of our home on the Gulf Production Lease two miles northwest of Sour Lake. My father was transferred to this lease in 1931 where we lived in a Gulf Rental house.

All of us boys through the following years took advantage of the convenient woods of the Big Thicket close by while growing up. Squirrel and deer abounded within this region. My dad had little time for hunting having to devote his time and energy in keeping us fed and clothed. When our duties allowed each of us slipped away into the woods to hunt or fish as the creeks and ponds scattered around the fringe of the forests had bass and perch a plenty.

Another incident concerning my grandmother, Frances Collins Loftin, passed down to us through the years is also worth repeating. Accompanied by two of her oldest children, Artist and Lydia, she took their team of and wagon and went over to Old Hardin about ten miles southeast of their home to purchase supplies for the family.

They left after daybreak for it usually took a full day to make the roundtrip but and somehow they ran into some delays resulting in night overtaking them when they were still two miles from home. They heard the panther first scream behind them then a few minutes later it screamed off to their right. The next time it screamed, the panther was to their right front, and grandma whipped the team into a fast trot with the fifteen foot cattle whip clutched tightly in her right hand.

About two hundred yards from their home as they passed by a large bay gum tree on the right side of the trail the moon suddenly broke from behind a cloud, exposing the panther crouched beside the tree. As they raced by the tree, she leaned over and snapped the whip into the shadows obviously hitting the panther as it screamed and leaped upwards along the tree trunk.

Reaching the house, she told grandpa what happened and the following morning he and an older brother took their dogs down along the trail to the spot where the incident had occurred and found the bay gum, which had claw marks ten feet high on the trunk, obviously made by the panther reacting to the whip laid on his backside. The dogs trailed the animal deep into the woods, but after an hour or so, they called them off and went back to the house.

My children and grandchildren who read this may now understand why I wish my grandparents had lived long enough for me to hear the stories of their lives in the Big Thicket. They would have been priceless.

I remember little about my grandmother Loftin but recall the evening she passed from life surrounded by her children and their families. She was a very opinionated person with a dominant personality. Perhaps this came from being the oldest girl in a family of thirteen during times when life wasn't very easy.

I thank her for pressuring my grandfather to move to Houston County in 1903 for if they had remained in the Thicket it is doubtful my father and mother would ever have met much less married, and I would never have made the stage of life.

In the home where I grew up, there was a portrait

of my Loftin grandparents on the wall of my parent's bedroom. They were around forty years of age at the time the picture was made. Grandfather was a handsome man with dark piercing eyes fine nose and a carefully groomed beard. The eyes seem to bore into you as you study his features.

My mother spoke respectfully about her father-in-law saying Mr. Loftin was a gentleman in every sense of the word kind and considerate of others never one to dominant or control a conversation as did his wife and most of their children. Grandmother Loftin was a good-looking woman primly dressed with her hair in a bun of sorts. The set of her mouth and tilt of her chin indicates a determined individual however if you look close enough you could detect the faintest trace of a smile.

After my parents passed away most of their personal possessions, including the old portrait passed to Leonard Harmon who continued living in the old home several years before selling the place. I often wondered what had happened to the portrait and assumed Harmon had given it to Darla, his only child, so imagine my surprise when Shane came back from a visit with Harmon with the portrait.

Shane said Harmon asked him to take care of it. He told Shane he had given the portrait to Darla, but somehow it wound up in an old trailer house he lived in after selling our parents old home on the Gulf lease. While searching for something in the old trailer house that had been used for storage he came across the portrait buried underneath an old weather-beaten mattress much the worse for wear as rats had eaten away some of the edges. He gave the portrait to Shane who gave it to me.

I was completing final phase of work on the Loftin Chronicles a genealogy of my family when Shane brought the portrait home. I was thrilled to again see the portrait of my grandparents.

I carried the portrait to a professional photographer friend in Waco, Cliff Shelley, who refinished the portrait placing it in a handsome oak frame. He also made several eight by ten duplicates of the portrait, which were given to my sons and later to kinsmen attending the annual Loftin reunion at Honey Island in 1982. Shelley did a beautiful job with the portrait, adding a brass plaque on the lower right corner with the following words: "Leonard Lee Loftin (1849-1923) and wife, Frances Abigail Collins (1851-1935) moved from Jasper County, Mississippi to the settlement of Thicket in 1872. Raised nine of twelve children in this area. These two pioneers and their descendants contributed prominently to the development and rich heritage of the Thicket, southeast Texas and our Nation."

During our Loftin Family Reunion at Honey Island in July 1982, I presented the portrait to the caretaker of the Big Thicket Museum in Saratoga in behalf of my brothers and sister: Leonard Harmon Loftin, George Calvin Loftin, and Margaret Doris Loftin Parker as a memorial to our parents, Leonard Harrison Loftin and Jimmie Lois Zorn Loftin and brother James Lee Loftin. The caretaker promised to display the portrait in a prominent place in the museum, which was undergoing new construction at that particular time. The date was July 11, 1982.

The previous day at the reunion the portrait was displayed bringing back memories for some of the older ones in attendance including Aunt Bea wife of Hector

Loftin youngest brother of my father. Small photos of the portrait were available for heads of families present along with copies of the Loftin Chronicles covering eight generations of our Loftin family. It was gratifying to see the older kinsmen read the Chronicles tracing their American ancestry back to the founding father in Virginia.

Through the years, it was customary for me to telephone Harmon my oldest brother who lived twelve miles from Saratoga. I often asked whether our grandparents' portrait had been hung in the museum. He visited the museum twice and couldn't find the picture and no one seemed to know where the portrait was.

During a visit to Sour Lake in 1987, Harmon and I drove to Saratoga and asked the caretaker a newcomer about the picture. We finally found it behind several other pictures in a backroom of the museum. The caretaker assured us after the museum was renovated the picture would be prominently displayed. Such plans for enlargement of the museum never materialized for lack of funds and within five years the museum was torn down. All of the memorabilia was stored in a small building nearby. A lady historian from Hardin County was given responsibility for dispersing the memorabilia to owners or kinsmen.

All of this happened without my knowledge since my brother was in bad health and not able to stay abreast of the situation. During a talk with George Calvin my brother in Alvin in passing the subject of the portrait came up. Seems he had recently had a call from some relative in Kountze saying she had been contacted by some lady in charge of distributing the memorabilia from the old museum to rightful owners. She wanted to know the owner of an old portrait of Leonard and Frances Loftin she had in her possession. This lady had been placed in charge of the redistribution of items from the Big Thicket Museum and wanted some member of our family to claim it. G.C. had forgotten our donating the portrait to the museum until I reminded him of the presentation in 1982.

I assured him I intended to retrieve the picture for safekeeping and wrote the lady in charge of the memorabilia informing her I would come for the portrait. In February 1999 after visiting Harmon my brother in a nursing home in Kountze my wife Sissy and I drove by Saratoga and met the lady in charge who gave us the portrait. It is here in our home here in Lacy Lakeview. The portrait along with the original will in all probability pass into the ownership of my youngest sons, Shane, since he was given the old portrait by his uncle.

The following information is the last information I have concerning the descendants of Leonard and Frances Collins Loftin and their descendants. Some of what you read was mentioned earlier in this history.

Paula Jane the oldest married Lit Swearingen and both are buried in Felps Cemetery. They had seven children, Lee, Nixon, Otis, Otto, Ada, Oney, and Ollie. Lee married Maude Smith, Nixon married Ethel Shirley, Otis married Ellen Dorsett, and Otto married Maude Garrison. Ollie and Oney died young. Aunt Jane died while I was home on leave from the Army in August 1944. She and Lit Swearingen's home was only a half mile southwest of the Felps Cemetery. She and Sister Amanda were the two children who came with their parents by wagon train from Jasper County, Mississippi. My oldest brother named his only child Darla Jane the second name of his favorite aunt.

The second oldest, Frances Amanda, married John Swearingen brother of Lit who married Jane her sister. Their children were: Clara who married Allen Whitesides, Earl who married Minnie Lowe, Abba who married a Munson and Ollie who died young. These two Swearingen brothers John and Lit operated lumber mills in the Thicket earning a good living for their families.

The third child, Stacey Artist, first born in Texas married Alice Marcontell. Their children were, Eddy who married Zena Meyers, Johnnie who married Lois Bracken, and Jesse who married Christine Cartwright. Uncle Artist had those black fierce eyebrows typical of most of this Loftin group. I remember Uncle Artist visiting us in Batson. With black eyebrows arched over his eyes and mustache drooping around his mouth, I recall him sucking hot coffee from his saucer with loud slurping noises. He was struck by a log truck while visiting a grandchild near Loeb killing him instantly dying a death similar to Millard a brother who was killed by a car in the Thicket. Uncle Artist only had one good eye the other lost when a milk cow swung her head striking him in the eye with a horn.

Lydia the fourth child died in childbirth when she was only sixteen or seventeen we are told. No descendants. What little we have about this lady was described earlier in this history.

Ezekiel the fifth child died young around six or seven years of age and most of what we know was recorded earlier in this history.

James Millard the sixth child married twice, his first wife unknown to the author however his second wife was Viola Collins a cousin. Their children were as follows: Gladys, Artist, Francis, Leola, George Leonard, William Bradley, and Eugene. Gladys married James Baer and their children were James Ray and Mary Frances, Artist married Estelle Kelley and their children are James, Lee, Jack, and Earlene. (Frances died early). Leola married twice, first a Bulay the family, who owned Bulay Honey Farms down near Dayton and Liberty, then she married a Trevathan and their children are Bill and Cynthia. George Leonard married Betty Joe Stewart and their children are Ronnie and Denise, William Bradley married Lois and their children are Debra, Diana, Jeff, and Donna, Eugene Loftin married a lady from Ohio named Madlyn Garrison and their children are Lisa, Patty, and Mark. Gladys, Artist, G.L. and W.B. have passed on as of this writing in 2009.

The seventh oldest child of Leonard and Frances Collins was Matilda who died with an illness while in her teens leaving no descendants. As was the case with Zeke and Lydia what little we have was reported earlier in this history.

The eight oldest was Leonard Harrison Loftin my father who married Jimmie Lois Zorn and their children were Leonard Harmon, George Calvin, Doris Margaret, James Lee, and Donald Howard (author). The next chapter is devoted to my father and mother and the family they brought into this world.

The ninth child, George Willis, married Sister Felps a widow who lived in the home of her parents near the cemetery and worked their old farm place. She was an independent woman and did the work of a man and perhaps for this reason she and Will did not get along too well. Will Loftin always had someone to care for him first his mother then his sister Paley When he and Sister Felps split up he went back to live with Paley his sister by then widowed with three children to support. He would live there the remainder of his life contributing little however Paley never complained and cared for her brother to the end of his days. Some bear greater crosses in life for sure.

Uncle Will was well known around Thicket calling square dances in the churches within the Thicket. He loved to dance, court the girls and ride horses which endeared him to my brother Harmon. During the 1960's During the 1960's Bill Daniels who had served as ambassador to Guam and was a brother to the Governor of Texas asked Will to drive his mule drawn wagon in the Salt Grass Trail Drives from the Big Thicket to the opening ceremonies of the Houston Stock Show. Will did this heading a long wagon train from Hardin County up highway 90 into the Astro Dome grounds.

Willis got along with everyone and was easy going with little care what tomorrow might bring as long as he had a bed to sleep in and food on the table. He did have some trouble with his brother Wiley Loftin who owned the house Paley and Will lived in. Through his generosity he allowed his sister to live there without paying a dime's rent. I know he was irritated over the fact Wills lived there without earning a dime or attempting to find work to help Paley with the kids. He and Will and came to blows a time or two over the situation. Each time Wiley got the better end of the confrontation. On one occasion Willis kept agitating him until Wiley grabbed him in a bear hug squeezing so hard he broke several ribs putting him in bed for several weeks. From then on, they stayed clear of each other.

We kids all loved to be around Uncle Willis Loftin because he was such a good story teller and always had everyone laughing. He always kept a good riding horse a high stepping sorrel used to visit kinsmen throughout the Big Thicket. He was the only member of the Loftin family to enter the service serving in the Calvary during WW I although he never went overseas. I have a picture of him by his horse which my father gave to me.

The tenth child, Willard Wiley, married Myra Rosier. Their children were: J.C., Arlen, and Jettilea. J.C. Loftin and wife Catherine had Triplets (girls). Jettilea Loftin married Leroy Hughes and brought into life eleven children. Arlen married a woman with two children as I recall. Myra Rosier Loftin was a sister to Lance Rosier who gained a reputation throughout the state and world for his knowledge of wild life and flowers (fauna and flora) in the Big Thicket. He was a self-educated person without a high school education but could name and identify every bird, flower and tree by its botanical name.

Lance often gave tours to naturalists on the staffs of colleges and universities from all over the nation. Roy Bedichek the famous naturalist from the University of Texas spent much time with Rosier in the Thicket drawing on his vast knowledge of the region. He is buried in Felps Cemetery a short distance from my parents and grandparents.

Sarah Paley Loftin the eleventh child married Ira Allemang and bore three children, Ira Jr., Jacqueline, and Frances. Ira left his wife and three young children when they were most in need of support and love. He dropped in every now and then to bond with his kids who never condemned him for his abandonment of the family. Paley's mother Frances Loftin was also living with them at this time and did until she died in 1934. Paley's life was one of service to others mainly her children, mother and brother all during the terrible thirties until all of her children were grown and married. Then she continued to raise the grandchildren and they were many from the marriage of her son Ira Jr.

Ira Allemang Jr. married a lady named Opal and she bore them twelve children. Ira like his father left home leaving his wife to raise the kids. He became captain of a tub boat in Louisiana and would occasionally come home to spend a day or so with his wife and children who thought he hung the moon. Ira died early in life around mid-forties and Opal never remarried but raised her children well with most receiving good educations and Arnold the oldest completed his education at TAMU and eventually became head chemist for Shell Oil Company in Houston.

The twelfth child, Benjamin Hector, married Beatrice Golden. Their children were Mildred, Bernice and Leonard. Uncle Hector farmed for a living until he was in his late fifties and then one day while clearing wooded land with a mule fell and broke several ribs. This put him in bed for several weeks during which time while reading the bible said the Lord told him to preach the gospel. Once on his feet he and his son built a small arbor along the main highway where he began holding services each Sunday. His preaching began attracting a few natives of the area and the offerings in the collection plate kept increasing until he and members of the congregation decided to build a wooden church. The church continued to prosper for a number of years until the old timers died out.

Uncle Hector bought a Model T Truck and began selling King James Bibles. My father gave me one on my twenty-first birthday. Uncle Hector often stopped by to visit while we were living there on the Gulf Production Lease. A likeable person and one admired by my folks since he had sense enough to quit trying to eke out as living in the Thicket and chose another much easier way to support his family named that of preaching and peddling products around Hardin County including bibles. He and Aunt Bea were real nice people a pleasure to be around and when we visited relatives in Thicket we always loved to eat at Aunt Beas since she not only prepared a delicious meal but kept a clean house. I think my uncle Hector passed from life during his early nineties while Aunt Bea lived into her early nineties before dying in a nursing home around Port Arthur.

They had three children, Marie, Bernice and Leonard. Bernice and husband attended one of our reunions in the 1980's and we occasionally shared correspondence. It must have been during the late 1990's she wrote to say Marie had died and her mother was in a nursing home in Port Arthur where she later died. Through the years since I have lost track of what happened to Leonard their only son. This concludes an overview of the family of my grandfather Leonard Lee Loftin most of whom sleep among the tall pines of the Big Thicket.

Only recently did I discover Leonard H. was living

in Thicket. Stan and I correspond frequently. Stan, his son, and I met on Facebook. I believe Leonard and I are the last grandsons of Leonard Lee Loftin and Frances Loftin.

Chapter Eight
Leonard Harrison Loftin*
1887-1976

Leonard Harrison Loftin was born May 11, 1887 in Thicket, Texas in the county of Hardin. He grew up in The Big Thicket with eleven other siblings. He was fifteen years of age when he moved with his parents and several of the other children to Trinity County in northeast Texas. The family settled near Pennington where my grandfather farmed for a living. This is where my father met my mother Jimmie Lois Zorn whose family were also farmers. The following is an account of their courtship and circumstances leading to their marriage.

They met while attending school in the one room school house in Pennington where one teacher was responsible for teaching all ages ranging from seven to nineteen. Older kids only attended school during the winter months since they assisted with planting and harvesting during the spring and fall.

As time passed their interest deepened but attempts at dating met with resistance from the Zorns who forbade their children from socializing with the Loftins. However, young love finds a way and they began seeing each other at parties held in the homes of friends. They made plans to elope when Mother was eighteen (Dad was seven years older.) since a church wedding was out of the question. On Sunday, September 22, 1912, they carried out their plan.

Mother went with her family to the Methodist Church in Pennington as usually and took a seat near the side door. During the service, she slipped out the side door and ran to where my father was waiting with a team and a buggy. As she climbed on the seat, Shelton and Gordon Zorn, her two brothers, tried to stop them but were restrained by Dad's two brothers, Millard and Willis. The Zorn boys were no match for the Loftin boys who laughed and held them until their brother and bride to be drove out of sight. Dad had made prior arrangements with a Baptist preacher and the marriage took place in this preacher's home that afternoon.

The Zorns were furious and refused to have anything to do with the couple. However, this changed in about nine months. The young couple spent their honeymoon in a small home on land sitting on the boundary line separating counties of Houston and Trinity. My older brothers said the home was in Trinity County and the barn and farm land was in Houston County. Dad farmed cotton in an attempt to earn a living which was the main product of most farmers in the area. This was a tough way to earn a living there in the red clay of the region.

Mother gave birth to her first child, Leonard Harmon, September 22, 1913 on their first wedding anniversary. The arrival of Harmon melted the resolve of the Zorns who had completely ignored my parents for the better part of a year and from that time on the two families were at least cordial to one another. My Zorn grandparents later said Leonard Loftin was the best son-in-law they had and did more for them than any of their other son-in-laws. I remember Dad always addressed my grandparents as Mr. And Mrs. Zorn. Of course they called him Leonard.

On July 24, 1915 the second oldest child arrived, George Calvin, followed by Doris Margaret January 25, 1918 as World War I was drawing to a close. Harmon had brown hair and blue eyes with a brown complexion and so did Doris while George Calvin was blond and fair complexion with blue eyes. Doris was really a beautiful girl with blue eyes. These three were born in Pennington while the family was in northeast Texas. Two more children would join the family after their moved to Hardin County in 1920.

By 1919, my father, finding it hard to make a living farming cotton in Trinity County, decided to move the family back to Thicket in Hardin County where he had grown up. He was confident he could earn a good living for his family farming or cutting and selling timber. So early in the spring of 1920 he and his brother Hector loaded their possessions on two mule drawn wagons and headed for Hardin County. Hector his youngest brother drove one wagon my father the other. The trip of around eighty five miles took about three days. Sixty seven years later in October 1987 Harmon my older brother and I visited the old Loftin homestead in Thicket where our father was born also the place where the family lived after returning from Trinity County. The home no longer was standing however Harmon was sure of the site.

Dad loved the Big Thicket and would have been content to continue living there, however, Mother who detested the Thicket refused to raise her children there.

To earn a living for his family of five, Dad cut cross ties for a seven mile stretch of railway connecting Saratoga with the settlement of Bragg. He received seventy five cents for each 8 foot tie. This was back breaking work with a saw and axe working from sunup to sundown.

Mother urged Dad to find work elsewhere so after a month or so he saddled his horse and rode ten miles to the Batson community where had heard they were hiring in the oil fields. Oil had been discovered at Batson in 1904 two years after the oil boom at Sour Lake and three years after the mammoth discovery at Beaumont, Texas. My father's first job was supplying hard wood for steam boilers on drilling rigs. He cut down trees then sawed them into firewood for the fireboxes on the boilers. He was paid three dollars a day working ten hours a day. He continued doing this until October in 1920 when he took a job with the Gulf Oil Company and moved his family to the Batson community. He worked with Gulf until his retirement thirty two years later.

On October 15, 1920, Mother gave birth to her fourth child and named him James Lee the second names of his two grandparents, Leonard Lee Loftin and Larkin James Zorn. On December 28, 1925 the last of the children Donald Howard was born and whom destiny chose to record this genealogy and history of our Loftin ancestors America. On Labor Day 1931 our family moved from Batson into a Gulf Rent House on the Tarver Hardin Production Lease of Gulf Oil a mile and half northwest of Sour Lake. We were now in the community where all of us children met our future spouses.

My father was moved to this production facility by Gulf to relieve vacations for lease operators while continuing to work as needed in the roustabout gang. Each morning, regardless of weather, he was up by 4:30 ate breakfast then drove seventeen miles to Saratoga to join the maintenance gang who would drive to one of the production facilities at Saratoga, Batson, Hull Daisetta and Sour Lake. I will never forget those cold winter mornings awakening to the sound of Dad cranking the old Chevrolet. The car had to be hand cranked requiring considerable amount of effort before the engine would fire up. If the crank wasn't held securely it could slip and break your hand or wrist. Some mornings it took several cranks to get it going but once the motor started he backed from the garage and took of down through the Jackson Creek bottom on his way to Saratoga. Some evenings he didn't get back home until after dark.

Mother's duties included getting us five out of bed, fed and off to school which wasn't an easy chore since George Calvin and James Lee always awoke in a foul mood. G.C. slept with Harmon and they usually had some words with each other before hitting the floor. Doris had a front bed room while J.L. and I slept on pallets in the front living room and during hot weather out on the front porch when the mosquitoes weren't too bad.

Doris helped Mother with breakfast and cleaning the dishes before leaving for school. I am not sure how the children got to school that first year. I was too young to attend. I believe they caught rides with some of the Jones kids who lived on farms three miles west of us. The Gulf Rental house we lived in was one of six facing the road connecting Sour Lake with Batson and Saratoga.

Across the road were open prairies broken up by vast stands of tall pine with hundreds of pumping wells and production facilities owned by the Texas Company the sixth largest company in the world. Growing up in these oil fields I became acquainted with the men who earned their living with these oil companies most of whom dressed in blue overalls and brogan shoes. Those were the days before hard hats were required so most men including my father wore old felt hats or oil soaked Stetsons. My father had a dollar and quarter Elgin watch tied to the front pocket of his blue overalls with a buckskin strap.

I would live on the Gulf Tarver Hardin Lease from 1931 until I entered the service in early 1944 and during those sixteen years became well acquainted with my environment, including the dense forests of the Big Thicket north of our home. I knew every pond and creek where the perch and bass lay waiting for a grasshopper placed on a hook dangling from a piece of twine. The marshlands north near the woods were favorite locations for wild ducks and geese during the winter months while squirrels and deer flourished the forests about me. I lived the life of the Barefoot Boy described by John Greenleaf Whittier in his poem by that name. I regret my sons and grandchildren were not able to experience the wonders of such an environment while in their teen age years however each generation is confronted with adjusting to the environment they find themselves in.

Several other families were living on the Gulf Lease when we arrived in 1931: the Rigg, Laughlins, and Kings. Homer Riggs, Cleo Laughlin and Perry King were lease operators along with "Judge" Norwell who lived in Sour Lake. We became good friends with all of these families however within three years all had moved or retired with the exception of Cleo Laughlin. Perry King was transferred to Gulf's operation near Batson.

When this move occurred, Dad was given his job as lease operator. These men were actually called "pumpers" however their job classification was that of lease operator for their duties were focused on keeping the wells and facilities in working order and the oil flowing into the storage tanks and from there into the giant pipeline tied into the Gulf Pipeline Station about a mile east of the field. By 1938 the Laughlins had moved to town leaving our family alone on the Tarver Hardin Lease. Our closest neighbors lived about a half mile from us and we kids either walked or hitched a ride to school.

I remember with great fondness picnics held by Gulf for their employees at Batson on the company's oil lease north of town. The men would barbeque a calf and several hogs all night and what a feast was spread the next day for families numbering around a hundred or more people. I can still smell the meat on those pits to this day and the large wooden barrels filled with lemonade and large pots of coffee. The tables were laden with all kinds of food. Also a string band playing in the evening while some of the people danced and us kids were running and playing.

I recall a young boy who played a large bass guitar in the string bane during the evening hours by the name of George Jones. During the afternoon before we ate there were games and contests one a 100 yard footrace by the men and I was pleasantly surprised and proud to see my dad had entered the race.

I had never seen my father run any distance against competition so it was surprising to see him line up with several other men most much younger. And to top it off he was going to race in his Sunday go to meeting shoes. I knew he was beat before they started. The gun sounded and off they went and by golly at the midpoint of the race my daddy put it in another gear and pulled away from the others winning by ten yards or more. I was thrilled seeing my dad win that race. What good memories of those picnics in Batson a tradition which was not continued by the Company in Sour Lake.

When my father began working full time as a lease operator he walked to work each morning. The production office was only about a quarter of a mile north of our house. On bitter cold mornings he placed newspapers inside his overhauls to break the biting cold. Leaning into the wind with one hand holding his hat on, he made it to the production office where he would check the status of conditions in the oil field.

There he met with the lease operator coming off the graveyard shift and received information concerning the status of the work especially if one of the pumping wells was down. If one was down, Dad reported this by phone to his boss Bill Moody in Hull Daisetta who would send the roustabout crew to get the well back on line. Dad loved his work as much as any man could love a job and repaid Gulf with unquestionable loyalty during his thirty two years with the company. I believe his pay was four dollars a day for five and a half days he worked each week. Not bad pay since a dollar was worth a dollar back then.

Dad may have missed work due to illness in his thirty two years with the company however I cannot recall this happening. This is truly remarkable since during the last ten years of his employment he was the only lease operator (pumper) on the Tarver Hardin Lease. Months passed without his supervisor showing up. He could easily have adjusted his schedule to take a long siesta or lunch break but after eating a sandwich he immediately returned to the job. He believed in giving a full day's work for a full day's pay. At the end of the workday, four-thirty, he worked in the garden and tended to the livestock and chickens.

Each morning he gauged the amount of oil in the five hundred barrel tanks and reported this to the main office in Hull Daisetta. If a well sanded up or a string of rods separated he called the roustabout gang to come fix the problem. Dad developed a great friendship with Bill Moody his supervisor. Moody sold Dad a thirty-two inch barrel twelve gauge Winchester Pump Shotgun which we all hunted with. The range of this weapon was something to behold.

Harmon was near eighteen when we moved to Sour Lake and a senior. Didn't want to move and told our parents how he felt. Indicated in no uncertain terms he wasn't going to move and preferred living with his uncles and aunts in the Thicket. He didn't get his wish, and Dad made him enroll in the Sour Lake School in September 1931.

He refused to take school seriously preferring instead to work cattle for some rancher in the area. They usually gave him a horse to ride but often took Sam our horse Dad used for plowing and farming. This situation would eventually result in a confrontation between my father and Harmon which grieved my mother something awful.

George Calvin was sixteen when we moved to Sour Lake and with his personality made new friends easily and became well-liked by everyone. Much like his Grandpa Zorn he loved to talk and would for hours if he could find someone to listen. Of course this was an attribute shared by every member of our family especially the men. During his junior year he fell in love with Eva Meyers a classmate and sister of Henry Meyers the school principal beginning a courtship which eventually ended in marriage.

Doris my beautiful sister a brunette with blue eyes took to school like a duck to water and was a popular member of her class. She graduated with honors then immediately married Ralph Parker and moved to Hackberry Louisiana where he was employed by W. T. Burton Oil Company. She married much too soon probably due to wanting to get away from the control of her parents who were pretty rough on her during her high school years.

Doris was a really attractive young lady with suitors calling on her for dates some of whom were much older which concerned our parents. When she failed to get home from a date before a certain time, there was usually a scene when she came through the door. I was rather young at the time but bitterly recall those times because of my love for my sister.

James Lee, around eleven at the time, quickly adjusted to school at Sour Lake and made good grades as well as becoming a member of the Sour Lake Warrior Football Team. He was well respected by everyone and carried the friendship of many of those classmates to his grave. He and I were the last members of our family to leave home. Since I was too young to begin school in 1931 I had to wait until the fall of 1932 to start. This gave me plenty of time to get well acquainted with my new environment.

My father built a pen to fatten his hogs about fifty yards from our back porch and near Mother's garden. The hogs were fed corn for six weeks before slaughter to insure the meat was firm. We boys had to hose the pen down every few days for Dad would not tolerate a sloppy environment even for hogs to be butchered.

Hog killing was a special time of working together resulting in good meat needed to sustain us during the cold winter months ahead. Mother trimmed pieces of meat from certain cuts used for making sausages. After grinding the meat into small pieces through a sausage grinder she mixed the meat with seasoning then force fed it through a sausage machine into small caissons made from small intestines of the hog then tied off and hung in the smokehouse. We ate fresh pork Mom fried each morning for several days after a butchering and was it good with biscuits, gravy and syrup. Hey, those were the good old days and we ate well. There was no television advising us each evening how poor we were.

Monday was wash day so named because it took all day for our mother to wash our clothes assisted by other family members to some extent. However she did most of the washing in tubs of water which was heated in the large iron pot in the backyard. This was the same pot where water was heated for scalding the hair off the carcass of the hog to be butchered.

Wood was the fuel used for about a year, then Dad

and the roustabout gang ran a gas line from the Gulf Lease to our house enabling us to burn caisson head gas not the cleanest fuel in the world but a lot better cutting and hauling wood. Dad converted Mom's old cast iron oven and stove to gas. She couldn't believe her baking turned out nearly as good as when she used wood.

It was hard to break old habits and customs but what the heck we were now living near Sour Lake. We now had electricity and stored the old coal oil lamps until a storm knocked out the power then they became useful once again.

Momma did the washing, however, we filled the pot with water as well as two water tubs sitting on a bench in an open shed near the smokehouse. There she hand scrubbed each dirty garment including Dad's oil soaked overalls along with the rest of the clothes in our family of six. One tub had a scrub board for scrubbing the other tub for rinsing. Then after wringing the water out of each garment she proceeded to carry the garments to the clothes lines Dad had strung between two four inch pipes on either end of the backyard. This took most of Monday, then the clothes had to be brought in, and she sprinkled the garments, which needed to be ironed the following day.

This was the work which eventually broke the health of my dear mother who went about her daily chores humming old church songs and thanking the Lord for her family and life. *I Come to the Garden Alone, Rock of Ages, Those Golden Bells* and so many more I listened to as a boy will always remain in my memory.

In addition to washing, ironing, sewing cleaning, working the garden and preserving fruits and vegetables for consumption during the entire year, Momma always prepared a good breakfast, dinner, and supper for us. We all sat down and ate together. There were no distractions such as televisions and no excuses to miss a meal unless sick. Momma also fed the chickens, gathered the eggs, helped butcher and smoke meat. And of course, she cared for each member of her family when they became ill with a medicine for about any ailment. I often lift my thoughts back to those days and think what an amazing person my mother was totally dedicated to the welfare of her husband and children.

The older boys usually helped Dad with the outside chores, and Doris assisted Mother with the inside work usually cleaning and ironing and such duties. Mom did all of the cooking consisting of preparing three meals daily beginning with breakfast for Dad then another for us kids before we left for school.

The afternoons were for baking, then preparing supper, however, she found time to spend reading her bible, sitting in the blue chair in the living room. The back-breaking grind began to tell on Mother as the 1930's passed and it was obvious her health was breaking. She never complained doing her work with a song on her lips singing and thanking God for His many blessings. She also managed write or phone her parents in Lufkin who were getting along in years.

Electricity was a new phenomenon we delighted in having so much better than the old kerosene lamps which were put away until storms would knock out our power. Mom continued to use the old wood stove until around 1944 when they bought an electric stove then a refrigerator to replace the old ice box filled twice a week by the delivery ice man. While the man was carrying the block of ice into our house we kids would look for chips of ice from the large blocks of ice beneath the thick blanket in the back of the truck. We usually got twenty five pound block of ice for our ice box sufficient to keep our milk and butter cool

When we moved to Sour Lake in 1931, all of the children were satisfied or at least tried to adjust to their new environment except 17 year old Harmon who refused to take school seriously and began leaving school during the day to work cattle for local ranchers. Shepherd the principal told our parents of his missing school and Dad threatened to give him a whipping but it did little good. His great love was working cattle from the back of a horse.

The problem that caused the final separation between Harmon and Dad happened one day when he used Sam our only horse to work cattle for some local rancher. On this particular day, Dad told Harmon to have Sam home when he got off as he had to break up a piece of land with a plow when he got off work. This happened around 1932 or 34 as Harmon was using Sam to work other people's cattle, which did not sit well with Dad. He couldn't see his horse and son working another person's cattle without some sort of compensation and he sure wasn't going to provide his only horse for a son to play cowboy.

When Dad came home from work and found no horse, he was one mad person. It was after dark when Harmon rode up and as he came through the gate Dad took hold of the bridle reins and told him to get down. He then said son I am going to give you a whipping. Harmon said no you are not. Dad then told him take a whipping or hit the road. Harmon went to the house packed an old suitcase hugged his mother's neck, who was crying, and began walking toward town.

Harmon and some local adventuresome young man about his age headed for New Mexico to work on a cattle ranch but ended up with some poor sheep herder back in the mountains caring for sheep in the dead of winter. Starving and freezing he wrote his mother to send bus fare which she did and he came home never to leave again with the exception of three years in the service during WW II.

When the fever tick showed up on livestock in Hardin County during the mid-1930's Harmon got a job as a livestock inspector for the federal government paying him forty dollars a month. His duty was to see that all livestock (cows, horses, mules, etc.) were dipped and or sprayed with creosote each month which was supposed to kill fever ticks on the animal. These ticks could cause humans much suffering if milk was drank or meat eaten from infected cattle, so it was important that this parasite be controlled and destroyed.

Harmon and other inspectors had to see that all such livestock be driven or taken to one of several locations about the county and there be run through a long deep vat of water mixed with the creosote mixture. This was a demanding job rounding up all livestock in the county and seeing each and every animal was dipped. Each animal had a green spot of paint dabbed on their shoulder while standing in the drip pen upon leaving the dipping vat. Each of the range riders or tick inspectors had to have a horse along with a truck and trailer in case they had to capture a cow or horse then load and haul the animal to the nearest dipping vat.

Several catch pens each with a dipping vat about

thirty foot long and eight feet deep had been built at several locations in Hardin County. One such facility was located a quarter of a mile east of where we were living during this time. Harmon had two horses which he rotated in carrying out his duties and kept his horses in the fenced in pasture where Dad kept his calves and milk cows. This was a terribly exciting time for me as I helped herd and drive the livestock to the pens the second Sunday in each month where they were run through a chute to plunge headfirst into the vat.

Few of the animals willingly took the plunge and had to be prodded with sticks or whipped with a quirt before leaping into the vat. People came from town to witness the dipping of the cattle and sometimes there were two or three hundred head of livestock in the pens bawling and moaning with men on horses working the cattle toward the chute. I had a horse named Socks loaned to us by Mr. Edward Daniel a neighbor and owner of the town theatre who asked Dad to keep Socks and see that he was dipped.

Of course we were able to ride and use the horse which more or less became mine to ride and care for. He eventually gave us Socks and for years this horse and I shared many wonderful times on the prairies northwest of Sour Lake. I rode him bareback with my legs clinched under his belly to hang on as we thundered through the tall grass and scattered stands of pine surrounding around our home. This tick law was in affect from 1935 to 1937 before the ban was lifted. Having Harmon back around our family eventually led to Dad and Harmon burying the hatchet and with the passage to time they were the only two members of our family living in the home out on the Gulf Tarver

Harding Lease.

G.C. made the transition to the Sour Lake School without blinking an eye and soon settled into the social life within as well as without the school. His problem was he was having such a good time dating he neglected his studies and failed his senior year. He dropped out and worked for a year with a Gulf States Distributor Agency then went to work for the Texas Pipeline.

He and Eva Meyers, a classmate, married in 1934 and raised two children George Jr. and Glenda Ann. I believe it was around 1951 when Texas Company transferred him to their Manvel lease near Alvin where they lived for a year or so before moving over to the Alvin community where they lived out their lives. Two more children Milton and Pamela were born to this couple while they were in Manvel. All of the children grew up there and married and have families of their own.

Doris married soon after completing high school in 1935 and moved to Louisiana to live with her husband. She and Ralph had one child in 1947 and remained in Louisiana several years after Ralph died of a heatstroke in 1961. She would eventually move back to Sour Lake after our mother's passing and proved to be a great support for our father in his later years.

James Lee and I spent more time together than the other siblings since we were closet in age. We had some good times playing there on the Gulf Lease during the thirties. So many experiences so many good memories. He had a small terrier he named or called Hunkus which he thought the world of. He was given the dog by Mr. and Mrs. Greenhill whose house we passed on our way to and from school each day. He noticed several new born puppies in their front yard one day and each day going home from school would stop and watch the puppies playing. One day while he was standing there Mr. Greenhill came out and asked him if he wanted a puppy and when the reply was yes told J.L. to take his pick. He chose the puppy he later named Hunkus which became his favorite pet and always at his heels. This all happened when he was still in the lower grades.

In his senior year he often rode Old Sam our horse in the evenings after school back on the northern reaches of the Gulf Lease with Hunkus trotting alongside. The extreme northern boundary of the Gulf Lease was separated from a cattle ranch owned by a Boss Dugas and on his property were several large water tanks where the livestock watered. One evening after making a ride he came home saying Hunkus had a running fit while we were back along Dugas fence line and ran through the fence and disappeared. I couldn't find her so she must have run into the woods nearby and hopefully she will be coming back home pretty soon.

Not so and the next morning instead of going to school (senior year) J.L. got on Sam and went looking for his dog. He came back around ten o'clock holding Hunks in front of him across the saddle. He found her in one of the water tanks floating. She had a running fit and apparently ran crazily into the water and drowned.

Dad told J.L. he had to go to school, but he refused saying he had to bury Hunks. He pieced together a coffin in which he placed his beloved pet and companion then went out some fifty yards north of our home where he dug a grave and buried her. My brother would own other dogs in his life but none received the attention or affection shown the little fox terrier. For years he kept her grave cleaned with rocks on it to keep varmints from disturbing the grave.

By the end of the 1930's J.L. and I were the only siblings at home. Harmon was gone and George Calvin and Doris married and getting on with their lives. G.C. and Eva had a pretty rough time during the first two years of their marriage and when their first born George Calvin Loftin Jr. showed up it became increasingly more difficult for the family. Things had gotten so bad economically for G.C. and family my parents invited them to move in with us which they did for about a year before G.C. went to work for the Texas Pipeline Company in Sour Lake and began drawing a regular check each month. He would remain with this company for forty five years.

J.L. completed school in 1939 and had gone off to college at Sam Houston State Teachers College the following year. Summers he worked for Arch Tibbets who owned a garage and filling station in Sour Lake. He continued this schedule and would complete two years at the college prior to outbreak of war with Japan in December 1941.

In 1939, Mother was diagnosed with diabetes by a Doctor Kaufman who had his office over the Woodall Drug Company in Sour Lake. She had gone to Kaufman who diagnosed her condition as sugar diabetes and told her he would start ordering insulin for her to inject into her system twice a day morning and night. J.L. drove us up to the doctor's office and waited for our mother to join us after seeing the doctor. We would never forget

Mother getting into the car crying and after a short time composed herself saying she was diagnosed with diabetes. We were not aware of the seriousness of the disease at the time but through the ensuing years witnessed the impact of the disease until it finally led to her death 18 years later.

Dad gave her insulin shots morning and evening prior to their retiring for the night. What an ordeal for both! The disease began to affect her eyesight to the point she lost most of the sight in one eye. She had been a faithful church attendee at the Methodist Church in Sour Lake since we arrived in 1931 however she began having to miss which disturbed her greatly.

Dad employed Mary an elderly colored woman who lived in the negro section of town. One of my duties was to drive over each morning and bring her to our house to wash the clothes on Mondays and then iron the clothes the next day. She usually came three days each week and was paid a few dollars. Mary did her work well. There were occasions when we could pick her up so she walked the mile and half from her home to our house and walked back that afternoon. This only occurred once or twice as I recall but for a woman of her age that was a remarkable feat. She thought well of my mother and our family. Mother gave her clothes as well as canned meat and vegetables for her family.

My mother's health continued to decline as we entered the 1940's with the war clouds looming in Europe as Hitler's armies overran Poland and Czechoslovakia. We all anticipated having to someday join England in her fight against Germany but kept praying this would not be necessary. We stayed out of the war until the Japanese hit our base at Pearl Harbor whereupon our president asked Congress to declare war on the AXIS Powers. This was done December 8 followed by another declaration of war against Germany and Italy the following day.

The die was cast and our family had three of four sons to enter the service. The first member of our family to enlist was Harmon in February 1942 followed by J.L. a few months later. Both entered the Army however after basic training J.L. was accepted in the United States Air Corp Cadet Training Program and after completing his training was commissioned an officer at Blackland Army Air Base near Waco in 1943. I write this from my study five miles east of where the Air Base was located now the Waco City Airport.

J.L. entered advanced flight training at Blackland to be trained to pilot B-17 Bombers. Within four months he was in Europe flying combat missions over Germany. He was assigned to the 534th Bomb Squadron, 381st Bomb Group in England. On October 9, 1943 while returning from his 13th bombing mission over Anklem, Germany his plane was shot down near Flensberg, Denmark. He was captured and spent nineteen months in a prisoner of war camp at Sagan prior to being moved to Germany's largest prisoner of war camp, Stalag VII-A, north of Moosburg in southern Bavaria.

Word of his missing in action hit our parents hard and to top it off Harmon was also in Europe with the 522nd AA unit. He was in the quartermaster corp responsible for trucking supplies and equipment to the front lines. I was working as a welder in Orange Consolidated Shipyards in Orange, Texas when word of J.L.'s capture reached us. I was called up for duty and was trained to San Antonio. On March 31, 1944 I was sworn into the United States Army at Fort Sam Houston in San Antonio and after completing basic training at Camp Hood Texas followed by amphibious training on the California coast our division sailed for Europe arriving in first week of March 1944. Our division completed the closing of the Ruhr Pocket then moved to the western border of Germany and Czechoslovakia and was in Marienbad Czechoslovakia when the war in Europe ended May 7, 1945. At this time our 97th was the 3rd Army.

Our division came home from Europe at the end of June 1945 and we were given thirty day furloughs during July. James Lee was home from the prisoner of war camp as well as my brother Harmon and we spent quality time together. We spent time swapping stories of our experiences. J.L. and I found out we both were on the Monticello which carried me over to France and brought J.L. home from Europe. Quite a coincidence!

I served as his best man in his marriage to Irene Swain a neighbor of Etoile Boswell (Sissie) who would later become my wife. At the end of the furlough, J.L., Irene, and Sissy drove me to Houston where I caught the train to Fayetteville, North Carolina where the 97th Division was preparing for departure to the Pacific Theatre.

While at Fort Bragg, the bombs were dropped on Japan cities and the war began coming to a close. We thought we would stay in the states, however, within a week, we trained to Fort Lewis, Washington and shipped out for Japan near the middle of August 1945.We continued on to Japan for occupational duties headquartered in Fukushima. I was there until the following April when I returned to the states for discharge at Fort Bliss in El Paso, Texas *May 1, 1945.*

The war was really a strain on our parents as well as others who had loved ones in the service, however, we were fortunate to have Doris, G.C. and their families at home to comfort and support our parents. Thanks to a merciful God we were allowed to come back, marry and raise children of our own.

Mother and Dad continued to live on the Gulf Lease and Mom a staunch Methodist made it to church while able. She loved her flowers and working in the flower beds in her front yard while Dad stayed occupied with his cows and chickens and gardening. He kept the front yard mowed with a hand push mower. Dad retired from Gulf at sixty-five after thirty-two years with the company.

I remember his last day on the job went about like any other day as he worked a full eight hour shift before making the walk home for the last time. He made one last stop beside a pumping well about thirty yards west of our house where a picture was made of him standing beside the pumping unit with his hand on the motor. Thirty two years of dedicated service and loyal to the bitter end. He loved Gulf Oil with a passion and would surely be in a state of denial if someone told him the company no longer exists.

Dad was so loyal to Gulf he continued trading with the Gulf Service Station in the community a competitor of James Lee owner of a Texaco Service Station only a block away. J. L. was upset with his dad for trading with a Gulf Service Station after he took over the Texaco Station from his father-in-law. Dad told him Gulf money allowed me to feed and clothe our family during some lean years and send you kids to school. I can't betray that trust. Gulf has had thousands of employees over the life of the company but none more faithful than my father.

Dad and Harmon went into the cattle business and fenced the entire Gulf Lease of six hundred and forty acres to keep their livestock from wandering into town. This was the result of a stock law passed by the state holding owners of livestock responsible for accidents caused by stray livestock.

It was not unusual for downtown businesses to have cows lying in front of their doors creating a nuisance for the owners not to mention the offal which had to be cleaned from the sidewalk. My father loved to be around livestock and knew how to handle cattle better than Harmon however through their efforts they gradually built up a nice herd of around one hundred cattle of Brahma and Jersey stock. Harmon and his wife Odile Jordan separated and eventually divorced resulting in the herd having to be sold and the profits divided. They had one child a girl Darla. What a tragedy!

During this period of time from the 1930's through the decade of the 1940's, several of Dad's brothers and sisters passed from life and was laid to rest in Felps Cemetery in the Thicket. He and the remaining brothers along with other kinsmen and friends spent one Sunday each month at the cemetery caring for the graves mowing the grass and resetting disturbed grave markers and headstones.

He and Mom were glad to have their children back home or near enough for visits during the holidays and pleased to welcome the arrival of their first grandchildren. As the 1950's began Mom's health declined rapidly especially her eyesight making it difficult to read her Bible each afternoon. Loved and respected by the people of Sour Lake she often had visitors drop by to visit.

During Christmas holidays 1957 our family came together in our parent's home on the Gulf Lease. Harmon, Darla, G. C., Eva, their children, George, Glenda, Milton and Pam, from Alvin, and J.L., Irene, their children, Jim, and Lissa. Doris and, Ralph and their son Jimmie Lynn came from Hackberry and Sissie and I and our two sons, Don and Tim from Aransas Pass.

We had no idea this was to be our last Christmas together as a family since Mother died the following May. We found a beautiful little pine on the prairie nearby which the grandkids helped decorate with old decorations Mom always pulled from the front closet each Christmas time. I am thankful pictures were taken of the family during this gathering. On Christmas evening, Mom became so ill we called for an ambulance that carried her to the Baptist Hospital in Beaumont where they drained the fluid from her lungs. This dampened our spirits, however, she improved so much we returned to our home in Aransas Pass. Within a week we received word Mom was back home and doing okay which was encouraging.

The families once again came together in Sour Lake Easter April 1958. The weather was nice all through the Easter week with trees and flowers in full bloom. Sissie, Don, Tim and I took Mother for a long ride through the piney woods north or Sour Lake in our new 1958 Chevrolet Brookwood Station Wagon. The countryside was never more beautiful with dogwood trees in full bloom. She seemed to really enjoy the outing. When the holidays were over we returned to Aransas Pass never knowing we would never see Mom again.

In early May word came that Mom was back in Baptist Hospital in Beaumont to have fluid drained from her lungs and lymph nodes. Dad religiously made trips to visit her each day except on May 20th when she called to tell him don't bother coming wait until tomorrow. The doctor says I can come home so bring me a change of clothes and I will see you in the morning. Words from an old song remind us that so often "tomorrow never comes" for some of us which was the case with my mother. The following morning around four a.m. the nurse making her rounds found Mother had passed away.

The doctor called my parent's home, and Harmon answered and after receiving the news called Dad who by then was on his way to the phone. Handing the phone to Dad, he said it's about Momma. Harmon notified J.L. who drove to Beaumont and went to her room where she lay propped up with one hand frozen above her head as if she was reaching for the emergency cord. She apparently was trying to ring for help when her heart gave out.

The last member of our family to see and talk with my mother was Odile Loftin, divorced wife of Harmon Loftin, who dropped by the hospital the previous afternoon around four p.m. and spent a few minutes chatting and later told us she was in good spirits and real anxious to be going home the next day.

I was in a motel in Pleasanton, Texas near San

Antonio when Sissie relayed the news about my mother. That was the first time I stayed at this particular hotel as I usually stayed at the Encino Hotel in Pleasanton. I checked out and headed for Aransas Pass where Sissie, Donny, and Tim were packed and ready to travel. We arrived at our old home place in the afternoon where the family had once again gathered.

Our mother's body was laid out in a casket in the living room and a stream of visitors came to pay their respects to this lady, a faithful daughter, loving wife and mother during her life span of nearly sixty four years. A faithful member of the Methodist Church she never gave up urging members of the family to attend church. I thank her for being such a good mother and instilling in me a deep love of the word of God in Holy Scripture.

We laid her to rest in Felps Cemetery May 23 in a plot Dad had chosen for them years before. No more pain. No more troubles. I believe Christ called my mother home to save her from further suffering which she had endured during much of her life. She was finally home among the angels.

My father, until the passing of Mother, seldom attended church, however, after her death he went religiously, never missing a Sunday. He became a faithful member of the Methodist Church, devoting his time and energy in assisting others in need of help. For his efforts, he received the first Old Timers Award given by the Lions Club in Sour Lake.

Dad passed from life May 22, 1976, eighteen years and one day after the passing of Mother. So Dad, at last, was rejoined with the girl he fell in love with and married in Pennington, Texas September 22, 1912.

After her death, he had contributed greatly to his church and those less fortunate around his town and Hardin County.

I believe after being more or less immobilized during the last two years of his life, he was ready to join Mom and await the resurrection of our Savior Jesus Christ. I only wish they could have known all of their grandchildren and well as our daughters-in-law. There is no doubt they would have had great love for each of them. Hopefully this wish will come to pass when we reunite in heaven.

My brother James Lee was the next family member to pass away June 22, 1979 at his home in Sour Lake. He was buried in Forest Lawn Cemetery in Beaumont, Texas beside Howard Swain his father-in-law. His widow Irene remarried to Sam Mixon after ten years but at the time of this writing they were separated and she was living alone in her home on Crosby Street in Sour Lake.

Jim their son led a hectic life after returning from Vietnam; pursuing one career path after another always a restless soul. We were happy to get word from Jim in early 2007 he was enrolling in Sacred Heart Seminary in Hales Corners, Wisconsin to study for the priesthood. He was certain he had finally found his calling in life however after a semester he dropped out and returned home where he lives today in a home near his widowed mother. He is back working in the business field and seems happy and content.

Lisa after completing LSU entered the nursing field and eventually became Supervisor of the children's unit at Methodist Hospital. I believe she still works in the administration of this hospital. She married Whayne

Harrison an engineering graduate of TAMU who helped design the nuclear facility in Brazoria County. Wayne and Lisa Harrison currently reside in Lake Jackson, Texas both pursuing their careers with no children. (Since editing this history last word reached us that Sam Mixon has passed leaving Irene Swain Loftin Mixon a widow for the second time.)

My sister Doris Margaret Loftin Parker passed from life January 29, 1993, four days following her seventy fifth birth date in a Beaumont hospital. She had suffered from diabetes much like our mother and had to have a lower leg amputated which eventually led to gangrene that killed her. Services were held in the Pace Funeral Home in Kountze, Texas followed by internment in Felps Cemetery between Ralph her husband and her mother. This only sister of mine meant so much to me while I was growing up during the 1930's. She had rather difficult life growing up between four brothers but never lost her great sense of humor or kindness for those fortunate enough to share her journey through life.

Doris left an only child, Jimmy Lynn Parker and three grandchildren, Theresa (Recee), Margaret (Maggie) from his marriage to Judy Ardoin and Jennifer from Noi a Cambodian his second wife. This marriage seemingly a good marriage went to seed while they were living in Saudi Arabia where Jimmy was employed by ARAMCO. These three grandchildren were raised by their grandmother Doris Loftin Parker in Sour Lake.

After Doris passed away Jimmy Parker entered the nursing field. I understand the two oldest are still in the Sour Lake Beaumont area while Jennifer is in Odessa

College on an athletic scholarship according to the grapevine. Word has reached us she now has great grandchildren who will never know the great love and kindness of this wonderful sister of mine. Doris life was one of trial and tribulation losing her spouse early in their marriage and having to raise Jimmie their son without help from anyone.

Jimmie was sent by the Texas Company to work in Saudi Arabia and eventually brought his wife and two children over there to live. Problems cropped up in their marriage causing the split up of Jimmie and Judy Ardoin his wife. After a few months the children were sent home to live with their grandmother Doris who actually spent the next fifteen years raising and caring for these grandchildren. She cared for these kids until they completed high school. What a loving mother and grandmother! I wish life had treated her more kindly however there must be a special place in heaven for my sister.

Leonard Harmon my oldest brother was the next member of our family to pass from this life. He died February 17, 1999 in Dubuis Hospital, Beaumont, Texas at the age of eighty-five. For the last year he had been confined to a nursing home in Kountze, Texas. Services were held in the Methodist Church in Sour Lake with many relatives and friends in attendance.

He was survived by his only child, Darla Loftin Wilkins Griffin, husband Calvin, four grandchildren, Shannon Garcia, Nicole Wilkins, Kevin Griffin and Bryant Griffin and one great grandchild, Brandin Monroe Biano. Harmon was a resident of Hardin County for eighty years and resident of Sour Lake for sixty eight years. They laid him out with his old cowboy hat and a blowing horn on his chest. He would have like that. He was laid to rest beside his mother in Felps Cemetery.

He was born a century too late and would have loved the great cattle drives out of Texas to the rail heads in Kansas. Seems about every time I called him during the last years of his life he was watching Lonesome Dove or some rodeo on t v. Augustus McRae and Leonard Harmon Loftin would have made a good pair to listen to around the campfires on their way to Montana. This brother was my hero as I grew up a real down to earth cowboy who loved to work cattle. With the big hat and those batwing chaps hugging his thighs rope tied to the pommel of his saddle he was something else.

I will always have this memory of my brother. He brought me a registered sow all the way from Pennington when I was twelve and gave her to me after I promised him I would never take up cigarettes. I kept this promise at least until I entered he service and started chewing on cigars. My dad had little consideration or concern for pets including hogs and after she had a litter or two of pigs Dad butchered my sow after a cold norther hit us in the mid 1930's. Kind of hard to enjoy the pork chops Mom prepared from my "pet" at least for the first two bites, but after a biscuit or two and sopping with molasses the memory of my pet sort of went by the wayside.

Ain't it funny how we tend to remember little things from our past stored deeply in our mind! My oldest brother was special for sure, carefree with little worry about tomorrow as long as he had a horse beneath him. His kinsmen aunts and uncles and cousins in the Big Thicket thought the sun rose and set on Harmon. Each time he dropped in to visit he would pass into the kitchen wherever he happened to be, grabbed a piece of cornbread or whatever was left from dinner along with a piece of chicken or beef and stand eating and talking until it was gone. He then went to the icebox took out a pan of milk or buttermilk and after drinking it walk back out to his truck say goodbye and take off. All the time carrying on a conversation with everyone until he drove off leaving those behind usually confused.

When Uncle Will an elderly uncle living with Aunt Palley in Thicket would get down with consumption and or just feeling bad from arthritis etc. he would drop by and slip him a pint of Jim Bean whiskey to sip on during those cold nights when the wind blew through those clapboard logs of the room where he slept and would eventually pass from this life. This brother was worshipped by not only my father's side of the family but the Zorns as well.

George Calvin Loftin died April 20, 1999, in Clear Lake Hospital at the age of 83. His passing occurred two months after the passing of Harmon his brother. He was survived by his two daughters, Glenda Loftin Crawford and her husband George, and Pan Loftin Goergen, and husband Jerry: by his two sons, George C. Loftin, Jr. and his wife, Theresa, and Milton B. Loftin and wife, Donna; all of Alvin by Donald H. Loftin and wife, Sissy of Waco: by six grandchildren, Jerry Wayne Loftin, Cindy Lewis, Byron Loftin, Leslie Crawford Tarver, Mysti Loftin and Jarrod Goergen: by seven great grandchildren and by a host of friends of all ages. Services for G.C. were held in held in the

Methodist Church in Alvin his body placed beside Eva his wife in Confederate Cemetery in Alvin. (Eva Lola Myers died November 7, 1986). This brother of mine went through life like his Grandpa Larkin Zorn never meeting a stranger. He loved to sit and talk as much as anyone I have ever known.

We had some great times together especially during the last ten years of his life the most memorable times spent hunting for squirrel and deer around the Black Cat Camp northwest of Sour Lake in the depths of the Big Thicket. Sitting around the campfire we talked long into the night often into the early hours of morning snacking on strips of barbequed venison. I thank the Good Lord for having the foresight to record those talks with my brother and captured important family history for our children and grandchildren.

G.C. touched the lives of so many people in a positive manner. A good man liked and respected by all was survived by three children, oldest George Calvin Loftin Jr. who died of cancer in 2005 leaving, Glenda Loftin Crawford, Milton Byron Loftin, Pamela Loftin Georgen, and several grandchildren in the Alvin area. They still live in that area of the state and through the years thanks to the computer we have managed to stay in fairly close touch through Glenda and Pam and their families. Hard to believe they are now grown with children and grandchildren to love and cherish.

With the passing of G.C. in April 2000, I am the lone surviving member of the family of Leonard and Jimmie Loftin representing the ninth generation of our family in America. My three sons, Donald Harold, Timothy Howard, and Shane Stephen are the tenth generation while my six grandchildren, Lance Tyler

Loftin, Timothy Cole Loftin, Savannah Michelle Loftin, Haley Ann Loftin, Hannah Marie Loftin, and Victoria Anne Loftin represent the eleventh generation of our branch of the Loftin family in America.

With this work the bridge is now complete, connecting my sons and grandchildren to their Loftin ancestors in America. The continuation of my Loftin lineage and name is in the hands of my grandchildren those living as well as those who may appear later through the sands of time. May God continue to bless and guide each of them on their journey through life.

    Donald Howard Loftin
    Bridge Builder

Don H. Loftin

Made in the USA
Middletown, DE
16 July 2018